Also by Brenda Hasse

<u>An Afterlife Journey Trilogy</u>

On The Third Day

From Beyond The Grave

<u>Young Adult</u>

The Freelancer

A Lady's Destiny

The Moment Of Trust

Wilkinshire

<u>Picture Books for Children</u>

My Horsy And Me, What Can We Be?

Yes, I Am Loved

A Unicorn For My Birthday

Until We Meet Again

~

Brenda Hasse

Until We Meet Again

Copyright © 2020 by Brenda Hasse

All rights reserved. No part of the book may be used or reproduced by any means, graphic, electronic, or mechanical, including photocopying, recording, taping, or by any storage information retrieving system without the written permission of the publisher except in the case of brief quotations embodied in critical articles and reviews.

The characters in this novel are fictional. Their names, incidents, organizations, and dialogue in this novel are either the products of the author's imagination or used factiously. However, the dreams they have are based upon the author's experiences.

Because of the dynamic nature of the Internet, and Web address or links may have changed since publication and may no longer be valid.

ISBN: 978-1-7347786-2-5 (pbk)

ISBN: 978-1-7347786-3-2 (ebk)

To Peter, who enriched my life from a distance.
Until we meet again…

Continuing Onward

My first year of college ended with a farewell to my Irish roommate, Mol. After shipping most of her non-essential items home and overstuffing her backpack, Jasper and I drove her to the bus stop.

He pulled his car alongside the curb and put it into park. Together, we walked Mol to the door. I sighed as I turned toward my foreign friend.

"Text me often and let me know that you are safe."

Mol embraced me. "I promise, I will. I'm quite excited to see the rest of the country."

"You'll be staying in hostels the entire time?" I always thought of traveling by bus and staying in rent-a-bed, communal hostel was risky and a little scary. After all, one never knows who they will be sharing a room with, possibly someone of the opposite sex.

"Wouldn't have it any other way." Mol turned to Jasper. "Take care of my roomie."

She reached upward to wrap her arms around his broad shoulders. He bent down and enveloped her small body with his arms.

"Absolutely. You take care now. Keep in touch and call if you need anything."

"Shall do. Bye." Mol squeezed my arm as she passed by me, opened the door to the bus station, and began her adventure. As promised, she kept in touch via text and the internet and shared her adventure with us until she caught a flight home.

Home for the summer, I returned to the job I had retained for the past few years, managed to take two online courses, and keep Mom's flower garden in order. Dad seemed different, quiet, as we watched a movie together one evening. He left the room and returned in a few moments. It was the third time he had used the bathroom within the hour. I stared at him as he sat in his recliner chair and put his feet up.

"Dad, what's going on? You don't seem like yourself."

"Nothing to worry about. Just having trouble urinating, but I've seen a doctor."

A doctor? Dad never went to the doctor for any ailment.

"When did you begin having trouble?"

"First of the year, but as I said, I've seen the doctor and he is monitoring the issue. He recently increased my medication."

Increased medication? A twinge of panic tightened my stomach. *Was or wasn't the medication working*? I kept the thought to myself.

"Why didn't you tell me about this before?"

"I didn't want to trouble you while you were focusing on your classes. Really, it's nothing. I'm just getting old."

"I don't think you are old."

My comment brought a smile to his face.

I saw Jasper as often as our work schedules allowed and we called each other daily. My relationship with him was pleasantly surprising. I'd heard of other couples having arguments or all-out 'fights.' Jasper and I were more like best friends who never argued. I wondered if others thought our relationship was unique or strange.

As my summer was ending and I prepared to return to college, I arrived home from work one afternoon to find Dad sitting at the kitchen table. He looked up from the paperwork he was reading and stared out the window at a bluebird on a nearby branch.

"Hi." I set my purse on the table. "Why are you home? Did you have the day off from work?"

"Yes, I had a follow-up with my doctor. He is recommending I see an oncologist."

My heart skipped a beat. "Oncologist?" I had to think for a moment. I sat down at the table. "You mean a cancer doctor?"

"Yes. My doctor suspects I have prostate cancer."

"So, it's not confirmed?"

"He's quite certain he is correct."

I wanted to cry, but I was too shocked to do so. Was Dad going to die?

Dad reached across the table and patted my hand as if reading my mind.

"Most men don't die from prostate cancer. It's known as a slow-growing cancer, but I won't know the extent of it until I see the oncologist. He or she will probably order a CT scan and do some further testing. Let's not jump to conclusions and take this one step at a time, OK?"

I tried to smile as I nodded in agreement.

My Junior Year

With classes resuming in a few days, I backed my fully loaded car out of the driveway and headed to college. It is strange, after routinely driving this same route so many times, how my mind seems to zone out like it is sleeping and awakens when I turn onto the main street of campus, astonished to have arrived so quickly. Parking my car temporarily in front of the dorm to unload it, I sent Dad a text to let him know I arrived safely before checking in at the front desk of the lobby and receiving the key to the same dorm room I had last year. I attached the key to the keychain to ensure I would not lose it before glancing at the clock on the wall. I wondered if Jasper may be at a morning soccer practice as I called him on my cellphone.

"Hey." His voice was raspy as if he had just woken from a nap.

"Hi, I'm in the lobby."

"I'll be right there."

I turned toward the sound of footsteps echoing from his hallway to see him jogging toward me.

"How was the drive?" He wrapped his arms around me and kissed my forehead as I returned his hug and stood on my tiptoes to kiss his lips.

"The usual two hours." We walked to my car and I unlocked the trunk. "Have you eaten lunch yet?"

Jasper unloaded three crates stacking them vertically on the ground.

"No, so as soon as we get your things in your room, we can grab a bite to eat. I have a second practice at 1:00, so I should have time for a quick nap after lunch." He picked up all three crates filled with my essentials while I grabbed an armful of clothes by their hangers from the backseat. I held the door open for him to enter the dorm. "Want to join me?"

I glanced over my shoulder as I led the way to my room. He raised and lowered his eyebrows teasingly with a suggestive smirk on his face.

"Tempting, but I want to get my room organized."

I juggled with my keys until I singled out my room key from the rest on my keychain. As I pointed it toward the lock, I discovered the door was cracked open. Pushing it with my foot,

UNTIL WE MEET AGAIN

I entered the room to see my new roommate sitting at my desk doodling on a pad of paper. She looked at me.

I hoped we would get along like Mol and I did. I had heard from Mol every few days as she traveled around the country. It was reassuring to know she was safe. However, once she returned home to Ireland, our communication seemed to lessen as we both had summer jobs. Now that we were both beginning another year of college, I assumed I would hear from her even less because of the distance between us, the time change, and our class loads.

I grinned as I stared at my new roommate. A proper introduction was in order.

"Hi, I'm Elizabeth." I opened my side of the closet to find clothes resembling the grim reaper's wardrobe. I pushed the sliding door to the other side and hung up my clothes freeing my arms from the burden.

"I'm Morgan." Her reply was monotone as she glanced in my direction before looking at the doorway as Jasper entered and set the crates in the center of the room.

I stepped beside him.

"This is my boyfriend, Jasper. Jasper, this is Morgan."

He nodded and extended his hand.

"Hi, Morgan."

She stared at his offered hand before shaking it reluctantly without making eye contact.

"Hi."

My first impression of my roommate was, how shall I say it, she appeared to be the polar opposite of me and a drastic change from Mol. Her entire wardrobe of basic black was accented by her ebony-dyed long stringy hair, tattoos, black lipstick, black nail polish, and countless piercings. I wondered if she was able to get through security at an airport without setting off an alarm.

I glanced toward the bunkbeds. There was bedding on the top bunk. Smiling inwardly, I hoped to have the bottom one this year and was relieved I would not be climbing the ladder every night to go to bed.

After unloading my car and parking it in its usual assigned spot, Jasper and I went to the cafeteria for lunch. His phone sounded as we placed our trays on a table in a booth and sat. He took his phone from his pocket and read the text before placing it next to his tray.

"Coach wants me to report to practice early, so I'll go there after I walk you back to the dorm." He bit into his cheeseburger. "I'll text you when I'm done with practice and meet you for dinner."

I scanned the cafeteria. For being lunchtime, it was nearly empty. Maybe many of the students were waiting until the day before classes began to arrive on campus. I liked to arrive a few days early to get settled, purchase my books, and walk the campus to find my classes before they started. I secretly hoped Jasper's groupies did not return to campus this year or at least ate in a different cafeteria. I was tired of dealing with that drama.

Jasper and I strolled hand in hand back to the dorm. With summer days waning, autumn colors painted the tips of the leaves on some of the towering old trees. We stopped on the sidewalk before the dorm. Jasper threaded his arms around my body as I reached up and cradled his face with the palms of my hands. He lowered his face to my ear and whispered.

"I love you."

I smiled.

"I love you too. Have fun at practice."

"I'll do my best." After a quick kiss, we parted ways.

I sighed as I entered my room. Morgan was still sitting at my, her desk. I opened a tote and began putting my underwear in an available drawer in the dresser. I glanced at my roommate. She was still doodling.

"Morgan, is there any particular way you wish to organize the room?"

She looked over her shoulder at me while continuing to move her pencil on the pad of paper.

"No."

"If you don't mind me asking, what are you drawing?"

She shrugged her shoulder.

"Whatever comes to mind."

"Do you mind if I look at what you are drawing?" I approached her desk as she handed me the sketch and several others. Most were animations, oriental cartoon types of drawings. They were quite good, actually very good. "Impressive. Are you majoring in art?"

"Yes."

"Maybe you would like to hang some of your work on our wall. I brought some picture hanger things that don't damage the walls. They are in one of my crates. I just need to find which one has them in it."

Morgan looked at her sketch as if judging it and back at me.

"OK."

I spent the next hour or so putting my things away while chatting with my new roommate. Most of our conversation was one-sided and I needed to prompt or pull answers from her while she continued to draw.

The futon lay in pieces on the floor. I found my screwdriver, plyers, and the sandwich bag containing the bolts, nuts, and washers, and got to work. When it was assembled, I pushed it against the wall where Mol and I had it last year. I set up my small refrigerator and microwave near my new desk. It seemed awkward to set my framed photographs on it and sit in Mol's chair. I set the vase of feathers in the left-hand corner of my desk.

The scratching of Morgan's pencil stopped.

"Wow, you must like feathers."

UNTIL WE MEET AGAIN

I looked at her. She was staring at my vase. I touched the glass exterior admiring one of the white feathers.

"I found the first feather on my Mom's desk after attending her funeral. I think she left it there for me to find. I've been finding them ever since. It may be silly of me to think so, but I like to believe whenever she is near me, she places one where I will find it."

Morgan was silent for a moment as if my reply was profound or perhaps too deep in thought for her. Her expressionless face displayed a glimmer of a grin.

"I don't think that is silly at all. I'm sorry for your loss."

I looked at her and returned her grin.

"Thank you."

My new roommate seemed nice and intelligent, yet she had a way of looking at the world differently than most people. A typical artistic introvert.

I convinced Morgan to join me for dinner. Jasper walked in later with the team. He was red-faced and his hair freshly washed. I smiled as he approached our booth.

"Hi, Morgan." He redirected his line of vision to me. "Hey, I have to sit with the team, but I can meet you back at your room afterward." He took a green bean from my plate, raised his eyebrows teasingly, and grasped my shoulder as he popped it into his mouth, kissed my cheek, and got in line for his food.

* * *

The next day, Morgan, Jasper, and I purchased our semester books and supplies, walked the campus, and located our classrooms. We stopped by the library too. I reapplied for my old job and was told I would most likely receive the same position since I did it last year.

The first week of classes was standard; attend class, do homework, eat, sleep, and repeat. It did not take long for Morgan to hang her impressive artwork on our walls, many of them receiving high grades from her professors. By the end of the third week, I began to sense a subtle change in my roommate's behavior. She spoke less often and seemed to withdraw further into her dark little world.

I entered our room after class the following week to see Morgan in her usual place, at her desk, but with her cellphone by her ear. She glanced toward the door as I entered, tears welling in her eyes. Her ebony hair flailed as she looked away to face the cinderblock wall. I set my backpack on the floor next to my desk and overheard her whisper.

"I gotta go, Mom. Bye."

She placed her phone face down on her desk and returned to doodling on her ever-present pad of paper.

I assumed she had an argument with her mom or was homesick. It was if there was an invisible tension in the room, uncomfortable, and I was apprehensive to break through it. Not quite certain how to handle the situation, I thought a change in the subject may be a good idea. I glanced at the back of her head as I sat down at my desk and opened my laptop.

"Have you checked out the activities and clubs they offer on campus. They are posted online and in the student center. I think there is an art club to join, maybe even an animation club too."

She shook her head indicating she had not.

"Would you like to attend Jasper's soccer game with me tomorrow?" At least attending the game would get her out of the room.

"I don't like sports."

Well, no one can say I didn't try. I thought of suggesting she talk to a counselor or the resident assistant but was afraid she may become defensive and withdraw even further.

I tried to focus on my homework, but I could not shake the feeling that something was wrong, kind of a red flag thing, where she was concerned. Maybe I could mention it to the RA? After mulling over the idea, I decided to stay out of it and let her handle whatever was bothering her. After all, this is college and she is considered an adult. I only had an hour before I needed to report to the library for work and I wanted to complete an assignment before I left.

Surprises

The heavy workload of my classes and the demand of my job at the library made the first month of my junior year pass by quickly. Jasper and I were together as often as our schedules allowed. I attended his home soccer games by juggling my weekend hours at the library. His groupies still attended his games. However, I was thankful they had given up their pursuit of him and moved onto their next victim. I called Dad several times a week. He had little to say about his health and brushed off the subject when I pressed for an update. I assumed he did not want to trouble me with the details.

UNTIL WE MEET AGAIN

Alone in my room, I turned the page of my calendar to see 'October' staring me in the face. I took a highlighter, outlined the square in yellow, and wrote 'Happy Birthday, Mom' in pen.

Jasper walked through the open door.

"Hey, what ya doing?" He peeked over my shoulder.

"Just marking Mom's birthday on the calendar."

He sensed my melancholy mood.

"Ah, good memories I hope." He kissed my cheek.

"Yes, always good memories of her. I just wish she were still alive, to ask for her advice, and spend time with her like old times."

With my roommate away at class, we had an hour together before Jasper had to go to practice. His next game was away. He would be leaving on the team bus early tomorrow afternoon and be gone for most of the weekend. I extended my hours at the library to cover for another worker, so I would be occupied throughout most of the time he was away.

* * *

I hovered near her door and watched as Elizabeth readied for class.

"The coming weeks will be difficult for her. When will it become easier?" I looked at my spirit guide for his answer.

"She still grieves and may do so for a long time. It must be remembered that her grieving is her love for you in which she has no direction to share it."

"Share it, you say." Her love for me is different from the love she has for Jasper. She needed something to fill the void in her heart. Something to care for and redirect her love. I smirked as an idea came to mind. Jasper. I looked at my spirit guide, who nodded in agreement as he understood my line of thinking.

* * *

The days leading up to Mom's birthday were filled with dread. As a family, we celebrated her birthday with all the fanfare we could afford; gifts, some of them handmade, dinner at a restaurant, and cake with ice cream once we arrived home. I often found myself on the verge of tears, especially when I discovered a white feather on the hallway floor outside of my dorm room today, the day of her birthday. Time is supposed to heal everything, but I think missing a loved one is not one of them. We remember smiles, laughter, and love. We treasure photographs and remember moments shared. We have little choice other than to keep pushing forward with our lives and hope to do them proud in our quest.

Jasper walked into my room in the afternoon carrying a shopping bag.

UNTIL WE MEET AGAIN

"I have something for you."

I looked up from the textbook I was reading while seated on the futon to see the bag in his hand and a devilish smile on his face, contagious enough to cause me to smile.

"What did you buy?"

He opened his jacket, reached into the inside pocket, and withdrew a short hair, white and tabby kitten. He sat on the couch and placed it in my outstretched hands.

I had been weepy all day and kept several facial tissues tucked under my sleeve and jeans pocket. Jasper's kindness pushed me over the edge as my eyes welled once again. I cuddled the kitten beneath my chin as my tears cascaded down my cheeks, unable to speak. His comforting arm wrapped around my shoulders gently giving me time to pull myself together. I wiped the dampness from my cheeks and held the kitten before me to look at its precious face.

"Oh, where did you get it?"

"Him. I got him from a shelter. He's a rescue. I thought it may be nice for you to not only remember your mom's birthday today but from now on you can remember it as the day you got this little guy." He stroked his finger on the top of the kitten's head.

"Thank you." I kissed Jasper before placing the kitten against my chest. His little body vibrated as he purred and rubbed his face against my chin as if thankful to have a permanent home. A kitten to care for was just what my soul needed. I looked at the shopping bag as it was placed on my lap.

"What's in the bag?" I peeked inside.

"The essentials; kitten food, litter, litter pan, scooper, and cat toys." He pulled each item from the bag proudly displaying them for my approval.

I looked around the tiny room.

"I guess the litter box will have to go on the floor on my side of the closet. His food can go under my desk." My eyes widened as I looked at Jasper. "Oh, I hope Morgan isn't allergic to cats."

"If she is, he can stay in my room." He winked teasingly. "I'm certain it will work out." He scanned the artwork on the wall. "Maybe it will give her something else to sketch."

We weren't allowed to have pets in the dorm, but we decided it was worth the risk. If we were caught, I would take him home for Dad to watch. The kitten would be going home with me during semester and summer breaks, so he would have to grow accustomed to living in two residences anyway.

I looked at his cute little face as I held him before me again.

"Well, we have to name you, little one." I glanced at Jasper. "What are we going to call him?"

"Max." Jasper petted the top of his head. "He looks like a Max to me."

UNTIL WE MEET AGAIN

My head tilted to the side as I tried to view his turned-away face.

"Max it is." I kissed the top of the kitten's head before drawing him near my chest. "We will have to shut the door and keep it closed from now on, so he doesn't escape."

We set up Max's litter box and placed him in it. Just like a pro, he knew what to do. His food and water were placed under my desk. We laughed as he jumped, tumbled, and batted his toys. Jasper left for practice and I returned to my homework while Max explored the room.

The door opened a few minutes later and my roommate entered.

"Why is the door..."

Max sprang from under the futon onto one of his toys.

"...ah, we have a cat." She looked at me. "Why do we have a cat?" She closed the door and looked down at the tiny beast.

"Morgan, this is Max. Jasper thought I needed cheering up, so he rescued Max from a shelter."

She stared down at the kitten.

"I'm more of a dog person, but I guess I have no other choice than to tolerate him."

As Jasper foretold, Max became the subject of her sketches. Most were drawn while he was sleeping.

* * *

I admired the vibrant autumn colors of the trees as I walked from the library to my dorm. I opened the door to see boxes on Morgan's desk chair and her clothes from the closet scattered upon the futon. Her artwork was missing from the walls and the top of her desk was empty. She dropped her books into a box and looked at me. I glanced at my bed as Max covered his face with his paw and continued to sleep on my pillow.

"What's going on?" I stood stunned with my backpack slung over one shoulder.

Morgan turned toward me with her fisted hand upon each hip.

"I finally convinced my parents to let me come home. I quit. College just isn't for me."

My eyes widened as I stared at the disheveled room.

"Have you given it a chance? I mean, it isn't even Thanksgiving yet."

"Dad is on his way to pick me up. I'm outta here." She pulled her blanket and sheets from the bed, lay them on the floor, and tossed her pillow in the center. She emptied her dresser drawers and the clothes from the futon and threw them on top of her pillow before gathering the ends of the sheet together and throwing it over her shoulder like Santa carrying a bag of toys.

UNTIL WE MEET AGAIN

I set my backpack on my desk chair and spotted an unfamiliar picture frame on my desk. I recognized Morgan's creative hand in the pencil sketch of Max curled up on my pillow sleeping. She had put the drawing in a dollar store frame. I picked it up and looked at her.

She nodded her head to one side.

"Think of it as a parting gift."

I grinned.

"Thank you." I hesitated to breach the subject but was compelled to do so. "You are such a talented artist. A college degree could open many doors for you. Are you sure you want to leave college?"

"Yes."

End of discussion. I helped her carry her items to the lobby. She stared out the window, sent a text, and remained silent while she waited for her dad to arrive. A car pulled up and stopped in front of the dorm.

"There's my dad." She tucked her cellphone in her back pocket and picked up her Santa bag as her dad opened the trunk of the car.

I carried a box to the car while her dad retrieved the remainder of her few belongings. After setting the box in the backseat, I paused to watch her toss her burden into the trunk.

I shoved my hands into the back pockets of my jeans and watched as she went to the passenger door and opened it.

"Well, I wish you luck."

She glanced at me quickly.

"Thanks." She sat, closed the door, and never looked back.

It was such a strange parting. I shook my head as I returned to my room with its upper bunk stripped and her desk, side of the closet, and dresser drawers empty. I went to the closet and spread out my clothes so they wouldn't get wrinkled anymore and moved my shoes to give Max more room to use the litterbox. I hoped I would no longer put on my shoe and feel litter beneath the ball of my foot. I had to give him credit. For being so little, he could fling it quite a distance.

I turned toward the door as it opened.

"Wow, what happened?" Jasper stood with his hands on his hips and looked about the naked room.

"My roommate quit and went home. I have a private room, at least for now. I doubt anyone will be assigned to it for the remainder of this semester. I just hope they don't charge me for it. It's not my fault she left."

Jasper raised his eyebrows and wrapped his arms around me.

"I can think of several advantages of you having a private room. We have a quiet place to study and more time for just the two of us, well three of us if you include Max." He nuzzled my neck as we joined Max on the bed.

* * *

UNTIL WE MEET AGAIN

The week before Thanksgiving break, I was studying in my room when Jasper walked in with a sly expression on his face. I had seen that devilish grin once before and knew he was up to something.

He plopped down on the futon next to me.

"Do you think we have room for one more?"

I scowled uncertain of his implication.

"One more, what?"

He unzipped his jacket. A tiny black nose poked over the edge of the opened zipper follow by the furry black head of a tiny kitten.

"I found him on the sidewalk. He came right up to me and meowed. I think someone dumped him off."

We were guilty of breaking the rule of the dorm by having a cat in my room but having two cats was pressing our luck.

Jasper pulled the kitten from the warmth of his jacket and placed him in my arms. It had medium-length charcoal hair and yellow eyes. I could feel its ribs and its belly was bulbous, a sign the kitten had little to eat and possibly roundworms. Its ears were dirty inside. Ear mites? It probably needed a flea bath. I held it at arm's length and could feel the vibration of his body while he purred loudly. Even without cuddling the kitten, it was happy and content. Examining its behind, I discovered it was a male, glanced at Max, who was waking from his nap, and hoped the two would get along. I looked at Jasper.

"How can I say no? He is such a cutie." I held him up to view his eyes. They weren't weeping any gunky stuff. A black cat? Some thought they were bad luck, but this one's luck had changed for the better. "What shall we name him?"

Jasper stroked his index finger on the kitten's head.

"I don't know. He is black, but Blackie isn't very creative." We both chuckled.

I knew what I didn't want his name to be.

"Not Satan or anything demonic. We don't want to give him a complex or hurt his self-esteem." I set him on my lap and stroked his fur. "His fur is so silky and soft."

Jasper stroked his finger on the top of the kitten's head.

"For being so tiny, he purrs as loud as the engine of a semi-truck." Jasper scowled. "A semi-truck's engine? I think they are known as Peterbilt engines. We can call him Petey."

I held the kitten up before me. His yellow eyes stared down at me, bulbous belly facing me, and his legs dangling loosely. I tilted my head to the side.

"He looks like a Petey."

"Then Petey it is. Petey and Max."

"I think it would be wise to keep Petey away from Max until he is cleaned up. I suspect he has worms, fleas, and ear mites. Let's go to the store and see what we can find to get this little guy healthy." I emptied a plastic crate of books while Jasper trimmed two paper cups for Petey's food and water. We put the kitten and his mini bowls on the floor, placed the crate over him to keep the kittens separated while we were gone, and set a stack of books on top.

I looked at Max as he rose from my pillow. He arched his back like a scared Halloween cat and stretched out his legs before jumping to the floor. He went to the crate and sniffed, but Petey was too busy eating to notice the curious intrusion. Since they were about the same size, I assumed they were close in age.

We were able to find the medications for worms and ear mites and flea shampoo at the store. We also purchased a cat carrier to transport them home during Thanksgiving break. Arriving back at the dorm, we used the large popcorn bowl to bring warm water from the bathroom and bathed Petey. He nearly tipped the bowl as he tried to get out of his bath by clinging to the side of it with his needle-sharp claws. Jasper held the bowl steady until his bath was finished. Once he was dried with a towel, we gave him his medications. He shook his head repeatedly and scratched his ears with his hind legs after applying the ear mite drops.

I placed Petey on the floor and we watched as Max approach cautiously. Both cats hissed, arched their backs, and the hair trailing down their spines stood on end like the quills on a porcupine. Their tails puffed as if they had stuck a claw in an outlet and received an electrical shock. I placed my fisted hands on my hips and looked at Jasper.

"It may take a while for them to get used to each other."

Within a day, the kittens were playing and wrestling, thankful to have each other as company. They curled into a knotted ball while they napped and made themselves comfortable on my pillow at night surrounding my head.

I returned from class one day, expecting the cats to be sitting in front of the door looking up at me as they usually do, but I found them chasing each other around the room instead. It was quite comical, and I laughed until I was paralyzed with pain as their claws pierced the material of my jeans and imbedded in my skin as they scaled my leg. Unable to retract their claws, I gingerly set my backpack on the floor and lifted each of them from my leg hoping I was not impaled too badly. I placed the kittens on my bed, unzipped my pants, and looked for battle wounds left by their claws. There were several scratches on my leg dotted with blood, but nothing too severe.

Leaving the room for a class or any other reason became a challenge with both kittens racing for the door to escape the confines of the four walls. There were a few times 'Petey the Speedy' had managed to scoot past us as we went to leave for class or to go out to eat. It was a comical race to see which one of us could catch him first as he scampered down the hallway.

I discovered the kitten's personalities were very different. Petey was full of energy and slept very little. Max slept a lot. So, when Max was sleeping, Petey expected me to entertain him, which made it difficult for me to study.

UNTIL WE MEET AGAIN

I especially liked to watch Jasper, my hulking boyfriend, handle the kittens gently. He often talked to them in a high-pitched voice and usually had Max on his lap while watching TV. If he stretched out on the bed, Max assumed his usual position cuddled close to his neck and purred. Max became his cat while Petey bonded with me.

Making Introductions

With my classes wrapped up for Thanksgiving break, I gathered my laundry and essentials to take home over the long weekend. Since Petey and Max were still quite small, they both fit into the cat carrier. I hoped by keeping them together during the two-hour trip home, it would alleviate any stress they may experience.

With my car loaded, I started the engine and looked at the cat carrier on the passenger seat as begging paws reached toward me.

"You're fine, boys."

Their constant meowing expressed their lack of belief in my reassurance. I reached my fingers through the holes of the carrier while I drove. Unable to withstand their incessant meowing, I relented and unlatched the door. Max climbed to the highest place he could find and still be near me, my shoulder. He widened his eyes and ducked his head as a car passed by our car. Eventually, he tucked his front paws beneath his chest and snuggled next to my neck. Petey preferred to settle in my lap.

Within a few blocks from home, Max began to yowl in my ear as if warning me of the inevitable. That's when I learned cats can get car sick. He upchucked the contents of his stomach on my shirt, much of it landing in my lap causing Petey to dart to the passenger seat and sit on top of the carrier.

When I arrived home, I placed both cats in the carrier, grabbed some tissue from my purse, and gather up the vomit. I planned to stock my car with facial tissues, a plastic bowl, baby wipes, and a garbage bag for the return trip to college, prepared to clean whatever followed his "I'm going to be sick" warning.

With Dad at work and my brother at school, I unloaded my car, settled the cats, and changed my clothes. I took a quick inventory of what was in the cupboards, refrigerator, and freezer as I called Grandma and made a list for needed groceries.

"Hello, you."

I learned in my business communications class to smile when talking on the phone. It was true. I could hear her smile in her voice, not to mention her never-ending energy.

"Hey, I'm home."

"I'm glad you made it safely."

"I have yet to talk to Dad, but I'm assuming we are coming to your house for Thanksgiving. What do you want us to bring?"

"Oh, I don't know. Mashed potatoes? I can make the gravy."

"That's not much for us to bring. I can make the pies and bring the whipped cream too."

"Perfect. I can do the rest. Oh, I have another call. Bye."

"Bye."

* * *

I entered the house with my arms loaded down with bags of groceries. Stepping into the kitchen, my brother stood like a statue with a kitten in each hand.

"What is this?" He displayed an all-knowing grin after stating his rhetorical question.

I set the groceries on the kitchen counter.

"I see you have met Petey and Max. Jasper gave them to me."

"Does Dad know about them?"

"No, but they are only here for the weekend."

"The weekend. What about during Christmas or your summer break?" He set them on the floor and watched as they scampered away.

UNTIL WE MEET AGAIN

"They will be here with me. I'm certain Dad won't mind. We have had cats before. Maybe he will welcome having them around." I silently hoped.

To smooth over the introduction, I had the table set and a nice spaghetti dinner ready-to-eat when Dad arrived home from work. Before I could broach the subject of the kittens, they came racing into the kitchen chasing each other. He looked down at their antics, briefcase still in hand, and smiled. He set his briefcase on the floor and scooped up a kitten in each hand bringing them close to his face. I took a small can of wet cat food from the kitchen cupboard and opened the top.

"The black one is Petey and the other one is Max." I divided the cat food between two saucers and placed them on the floor, my strategy was to fill their bellies so they would nap while we ate. Dad set each kitten before a dish.

"You will have to tell me all about them while we eat." He looked at the table. "Spaghetti, my favorite."

* * *

Potatoes mashed. Pies made. Canisters of whipped cream packed in a bag along with plastic containers for leftovers. Grandma greeted us at her back door dressed in her Thanksgiving themed apron.

"Happy Thanksgiving." She grinned from ear to ear.

I reheated the potatoes in the microwave and scooped it into the dish Grandma set out for it to be served. I helped dish up the rest of the food and place it on the table. We held hands and said grace before Dad carved the turkey. I looked at the table burdened with plates.

"There's so much food. It all looks so delicious. I don't know what to eat first."

My brother grabbed the mashed potatoes.

"An easy choice for me." He scooped several spoonfuls onto his plate and smothered it with gravy.

Since Grandma lived alone, having company for the holiday was a welcomed distraction even though she claimed to be busier than ever since her retirement. She talked incessantly while the rest of us ate with each of us adding to her mostly one-sided conversation whenever she took a bite to eat.

I promise myself not to eat to the point where my stomach hurt. Since the homecooked food was a vast improvement from the cafeteria food, I failed to abide by it. My stomach ached satisfactorily as I finished my last bite of turkey and cranberries.

Dad dismissed himself to the couch. Moments later his snoring resonated throughout the room. I do not know which one was louder, Dad's snoring or the volume of the TV my brother turned up to drown him out. Grandma and I cleaned up the kitchen and divided leftovers into containers. She got out some old photo albums and we sat at the table to look through them. There was a story behind every picture, and she wanted to ensure I knew each one. When Dad woke from his nap, we had dessert. He appeared groggy and tired. I assumed it was the effect of eating too much turkey, but then I noticed he went to bed shortly after we arrived home at eight o'clock.

The next afternoon, I took a break from preparing for finals to put up our Christmas decorations. Dad walked into the living room as I brought the boxes from the basement and set them on the living room floor. After removing the sections of the artificial Christmas tree from the box, the curious kittens appeared. Max sniffed the box hesitantly as if it may harm him. Petey hopped inside, crouched down, and sprang up batting Max's ear. It was all the encouragement timid Max needed. He jumped over the side of the box on top of Petey and began to wrestle.

Dad and I assembled the tree. He paused to watch the kittens play in the box while I fluffed and straightened the small wire branches and looked back at the tree in contemplation.

"I'll get the hammer, nails, and wire. As much energy as these two have, they will tip the tree over, ornaments and all." He insisted as he left the room.

The hair along Max's spine rose as he stared in the direction of the hammer hitting a nail. Dad pounded a second on the opposite side of the windowsill, wrapped a wire around the center of the tree and each nail. He reached inside the tree, grabbed the trunk, and gave it a shake.

"There, that should hold it steady."

I retrieved the strings of lights from a box and plugged each of them in the electrical outlet to ensure they lit while Dad added the angel to the top of the tree.

"There, my job is done." He brushed the palms of his hands together as if proud of his accomplishment, turned on the TV, and changed the channel to watch a sports station from his favorite chair.

I coiled a string of lights around the top of the tree while fighting off a never-ending attack from Petey. Unable to proceed any further, I untangled him from the lights and placed him in an empty box only to have him jump out and lunge at the end of the moving string of lights once again. Max sat dumbfounded as if entertained by my struggle.

I stepped back to view the lights and verify the tree was evenly lit. Satisfied, I opened a box of ornaments. Most were handmade by my brother or myself during our elementary school years. Some were made with Mom on snowy days when we didn't have school. I selected one and attached it to a branch. Noticing an unusual silence, I looked at the box to find it empty. I selected another ornament and placed its hook on a branch as a little black paw reached through the branches and batted it until it swung from side to side. I peeked into the Christmas tree to see two yellow eyes staring back at me.

"What are you doing in there?"

Petey batted at my nose.

UNTIL WE MEET AGAIN

I hung and secured the remaining ornaments by pinching each hook onto a branch. Max sat in the empty box watching my every movement. I stepped back to admire my work before spreading the tree skirt beneath it. It would only be a matter of time until Petey or Max dove beneath it chasing an imaginary mouse or lost cat toy. The tree's branches trembled as Petey moved from branch to branch. Every once and awhile, his paw would reach through the branches to bat at an ornament.

I hung the Christmas stockings, including Mom's stocking in memory of her. I like to believe she came to visit us to celebrate the holiday. I also set up the manger hoping the cats would leave the figures alone.

I turned to see my energetic kitten emerge from beneath the tree. His teeth simultaneously clenched a handmade green pipe cleaner wreath decorated with red beads and a string of lights.

"Petey, no!" I advanced toward him hoping to avoid any damage to the tree decorations.

In his panic, he pulled the wreath as he darted away. Unfortunately, Petey had also clamped down on a string of lights, ripping it from the tree, and causing several decorations to strip away from the branches and fall to the carpet as he released the ornament and hid under the tree.

Dad chuckled as he watched the kitten creep low to the floor to retrieve the tiny wreath and disappear beneath the branches. I stared at the drooping string of lights and ornaments on the floor. My brother came down from his room.

"What the heck is going on?"

I looked at him as he stood near Dad's chair with an inquisitive expression on his face.

"The demon cat tried to get an ornament from the tree and took a number of them and part of the lights with him." I motioned at the mess. "He likes the wreath you made in first grade."

Between my brother and I, it did not take long for us to redecorate the tree. We let Petey keep the ornament hoping he would leave the remainder of the tree alone.

* * *

We rose early Sunday morning, drank a quick cup of coffee, and went to church. After Mass, we sat at our usual table in the hall and enjoyed our favorite donuts. Grandma paused as she stood behind my chair carrying a cup of coffee in one hand and a donut on a napkin in the other. She leaned toward us.

"Would everyone like to stop by my house later for a light lunch?" She waited for our reply.

I did not want to disappoint her, but I planned to leave for college shortly after we returned home.

"Sorry, Grandma, but I need to get back to campus."

She tried to cover her disappointment with a smile.

"That's quite all right. Another time." She joined her friends at their usual table.

I sat in the passenger seat and glanced over my shoulder at my brother, who was playing a video game on his phone. I looked at Dad as he drove. He seemed different. He was withdrawn and less engaged in conversations during my weekend home. I decided to inquire about a topic he had yet to bring up.

"So, Dad, what's the update from the doctor?" His grip on the steering wheel tightened and he took a deep breath. I suspected he was keeping something from me and assumed he did not want to trouble me with the details or distract me from my studies.

"I have an appointment this week to go over the results of the CT scan. The doctor is quite certain I have prostate cancer. The question is what type and how far it may have spread."

"Spread?"

"Yes, or it could be contained within it. The CT scan will give us that answer."

"When do you see him?"

"On Thursday."

"I want you to call me that night with the results."

We pulled into the driveway. He looked at me as we waited for the garage door to open.

"There is nothing to worry about until we get the results. OK?"

"OK." For some reason, I wasn't so sure.

Petey and Max were waiting by the back door as we entered. I was eager to return to college, so I loaded my car with my clean clothes, leftovers from Thanksgiving, and the cats in their carrier, even though I knew they would not remain inside it during the entire two hours. I said my good-byes and reminded Dad to call me.

As expected, Max didn't get sick until I turned onto the main road of campus, just short of my destination. Thank goodness I was prepared.

*　*　*

With exams in a week, studying for them was difficult with Dad's diagnosis haunting my mind.

As promised, my cell phone rang Thursday night while Jasper and I were reviewing for our exams in my room.

"Hi, Dad." I stood from the futon and crossed the room.

"Hello, Elizabeth."

I wasn't in the mood for small talk.

"Well, what did the doc say?"

"My PSA is quite high. He is prescribing female hormones. I may become emotional at times and possibly grow breasts." He tried to downplay the severity by laughing. "I hope they don't get so large that I will have to wear a bra."

I wasn't laughing.

"Why is he having you take them?

"To slow the cancer growth."

My heartbeat increased. I assumed my blood pressure did as well. Need I pull the information from him? Was he avoiding the truth to protect me? Good news or bad, I needed to know.

"Did he review the scan with you?"

I heard him sigh.

"The CT scan indicates the cancer is outside of my prostate. It is in my hip and spine as well."

I looked at Jasper, who remained on the futon. He was staring at me. His eyebrows raised, questioning. I shook my head indicating the unfavorable results.

"So, the only plan is for you to take hormones? No chemo?"

"He wants to see if this remedy will lower my PSA and slow the cancer growth. Other options are being discussed."

"When do you start taking the hormones?"

"I began today, so expect me to be sensitive and weepy."

"Well, keep me posted."

"I will. I love you."

"I love you too, Dad. Bye."

"Good-bye, honey."

My eyes welled with tears as I turned toward my desk, set my phone down, and took a tissue from the box. Jasper's arms wrapped around my waist as he placed his chin gently on my shoulder.

* * *

I wanted to reach out and hold my daughter, to take away what troubled her.

"I dislike seeing her sad." I looked at my spirit guide.

"*She is worried.*"

"I'm thankful that is one emotion you leave behind when you depart from the physical world."

* * *

I dabbed the tears from the corner of my eyes and blew my nose before turning to face Jasper.

"It doesn't look good. His cancer has spread outside his prostate and it's in his hip and spine as well."

He brushed a strand of my hair away from my eye.

"Are they going to do chemo?"

"Not right now. He is undergoing hormone treatment, female hormones of some kind. He wasn't specific. There may be a few side effects like growing breasts, and he may become excessively emotional. The doctor is weighing other options if this doesn't work."

Jasper sighed.

"At least the doctor is being proactive."

"Maybe he knows the hormone treatment will be unsuccessful."

"You think? Or he may find a new treatment with a higher success rate."

"I don't know what to think. All I know is that I have to get through these exams and get home for Christmas break." I returned to the futon and tried to focus on my notes. Thoughts of going home, of caring for Dad monopolized my mind. As Jasper sat, I sprang up and retrieved my phone from my desk and made a call to my brother.

"Hey."

I could hear a video game playing in the background.

"Hey, are you in your room?"

"Ya."

"How's Dad?"

"He seems fine."

"Well, he isn't fine. Can you keep an eye on him?"

"Sure."

"I mean, spend more time with him. Make sure he is eating well too."

"I will. When are you coming home?"

"I'll be home in a week or so, depending on when my last exam is scheduled. Bye."

"Bye."

* * *

Exams were hell. My lack of concentration made them all the worse. Jasper, the cats, and I celebrated Christmas together before we parted for semester break. We were 'college poor' as they say, so we bought each other inexpensive presents. Petey received a package of pipe cleaners. Jasper and I twisted each one into a circle just like the pipe cleaner ornament he liked to play with at home. Max preferred to play with his gift, a bag of plastic balls with a jingle bell inside each one.

Once home for the holiday break, I baked cookies, made fudge, and wrapped my gifts. We attended midnight Mass and slept midway through the morning on Christmas day. Grandma joined us for dinner which included ham, cheesy potatoes, and all the fixings. We enjoyed my cookies and fudge for dessert. I could tell by the way she watched Dad she was concerned about his health too.

The following week, I insisted on accompanying him to his oncologist appointment. He simply nodded knowing I would argue if he fought the issue.

They drew blood, recorded his vitals, and asked a bunch of questions. I stepped into the hallway as the doctor checked the size of Dad's prostate. We were escorted to the oncologist's office and each sat in a chair before the mahogany desk. The doctor entered the room with a file under his arm, sat at his desk, and opened the file.

"Your PSA is down. How are you feeling?" He looked at Dad.

"To tell you the truth, I've never cried through so many movies in my life. I'm tired, but I have been able to continue to work."

The doctor looked down at the paperwork and nodded his head slightly.

"Since hormone therapy is keeping your PSA number in check, we will continue with the same dose. If the number increases, then we will look at other options."

Other options? My stomach tightened. If Dad's health took a turn for the worst, he meant. I leaned forward in my chair.

"What options?"

The doctor glanced at Dad before looking at me.

"There are several, chemotherapy, radiation, surgery, and experimental drugs. When the time comes, those options will be entertained."

"So, you're telling me he isn't going to get well." I took a deep breath to calm my quivering voice, but it raised an octave when I spoke. "That he is going to die?"

The doctor sighed as he clasped his hands together and placed them on the paperwork.

"Each case is different because each person is different. The type of cancer your father has is aggressive. It has already spread to other parts of his body. My plan of treatment is to take one day at a time, see what works and what doesn't work, and guide him to make the best decisions for his case." The doctor displayed a half-grin to convey what little hope he had to offer.

Dad reached and clasped my forearm resting on the armrest of the chair.

"We don't want to take up any more of the doctor's time. We can talk in the car." He rose and shook hands with the doctor.

I sat stupefied, realizing the answer to my question had been avoided for the very reason I dreaded. I struggled to keep my emotions in check as I sat in the passenger seat of the car and Dad got behind the steering wheel. He looked at me as I stared forward at nothing. I was afraid to look at him in fear of bursting into tears.

"Elizabeth, I know the news isn't good and my future isn't bright, but I also know I'm not going to die tomorrow. I'm going to fight this with everything I have in me. I need you to stay positive, hopeful, and pray."

I nodded my head, unable to speak.

* * *

UNTIL WE MEET AGAIN

With Christmas break over, Max, Petey, and I headed back to college to begin the second semester. Without a roommate assigned to share my room, it was reclassified as private. Just what I needed, more college debt upon graduation.

After our first day of class, Jasper and I snuggled on the futon while watching TV. Petey managed to settle himself on the edge of the cushion behind my neck. Jasper petted Max as he lay curled in his lap sleeping. My sentimental boyfriend leaned toward me and kissed my cheek, picked up my hand, wove his fingers between mine, and placed a kiss beneath my knuckles.

"I love you."

I looked at him and smirked.

"I love you too." There was a playfulness in his voice, so I thought he was kidding.

"No, I really love you."

I looked at his serious face a bit puzzled. My grin faded.

"And I really love you."

"Enough to spend the rest of your life with me?"

I didn't know what to think. I never entertained the thought much. I mean, it had crossed my mind, but I was only 19, soon to turn 20. In my opinion, too young to get married. Maybe I wasn't ready for that big of a step in my life. I certainly didn't think he was. We had to finish college and I planned to get my master's degree in business. I decided to share my opinion on the subject honestly.

"It has crossed my mind, but my concern for Dad and school has taken precedence."

He tilted his head and scowled.

"So, you're saying you wouldn't want to marry me?"

I sighed.

"No, I would want to marry you, just not right now. We both have another year of school and I have Dad to worry about."

"So, you want to marry me?"

I had the impression he was fishing for an answer.

"Yes, someday."

He wrapped his arm around my shoulder and pulled me near him.

"Good." He nodded his head before focusing on the TV show.

* * *

I spoke to Dad several times a week with the hope of monitoring his health and keeping his spirits high. He called me in the evenings after each oncologist appointment with an update. It was a relief to hear his PSA number continued to stay low and stable. The hormones affected his emotions greatly. During several conversations, he sobbed over the silliest things; memories of Mom, something that happened at work, and

UNTIL WE MEET AGAIN

explaining a sentimental scene from a movie. Welcome to womanhood, Dad.

My Last Summer Break

The daffodils were in full bloom and the tulips ready to burst open with their vibrant colors. I packed up my room, headed home, and returned to my job with a heavy load of online summer classes scheduled. Even though Dad's health was stable, I was afraid he may take a turn for the worse and I would have to leave school my senior year before finishing my degree.

I requested a flexible work schedule so I could attend most of Dad's doctor appointments. He seemed to be doing well. However, it was becoming uncomfortable for him to sit.

I drove him to his next oncologist appointment. He had his blood drawn and was examined while I waited in the waiting room. I was ushered into the doctor's private office and joined him for the consultation. The doctor looked down at the open file on his desk.

"Your PSA rose slightly last month but remains in the normal range. Your prostate has increased in size and is the reason it's uncomfortable for you to sit." He looked at Dad. "Once I receive the results from today's bloodwork, we can determine where to go from there."

I took a deep breath gathering my courage, hoping to be brave.

"So, this is when we entertain other options."

The doctor looked at me.

"The bloodwork results should be back in a week. We can determine where to go from there."

I dislike when someone repeats what they said as if I was too stupid to understand it when they said it the first time.

We returned to the doctor the next week. As he predicted, Dad's PSA had risen. Since he was becoming more uncomfortable when sitting, the doctor recommended surgery to have his prostate removed. He went on to explain most prostates are removed robotically, but Dad was not a candidate because of his age. Furthermore, the doctor indicated he could not do the surgery and referred us to a female oncologist. We waited by the front desk for the secretary to make an appointment with the new doctor. She handed Dad the reminder card. I glanced at the date. His appointment was three weeks away. I wondered how much his cancer would grow during that time, increasing his inability to sit for lengths of time.

The new oncologist was nice. We sat before the female doctor waiting for her opinion as she scanned Dad's file. She assumed the reason the male doctors refuse to do the surgery was that their hands may be too large to navigate in a small area. She held up her dainty hands in order to convince Dad of her capability.

"Just because they are small, doesn't mean they aren't strong and capable." She lowered her hands. "The surgery has repercussions though." She went onto explain Dad would experience incontinence and more than likely need to wear adult diapers for the remainder of his life.

He shifted his weight from one hip to the other and looked at me as if silently asking my opinion. I gave Dad a nod of encouragement. He looked at the doctor.

"Well, I would like to sit comfortably in my favorite chair once again. Let's schedule the surgery."

His surgery was scheduled, but it was two months away. Again, I could not help but wonder how much the merciless cancer would spread during that time even though he continued with hormone therapy. It seemed as if there was no sense of urgency on either doctor's conscious.

It was the first Tuesday in August when I drove Dad to the hospital for his surgery. We arrived early in the morning, prepped, and ready to go. I kissed him on the cheek as he was wheeled into surgery. I went to the waiting room hoping to focus on the two remaining online classes I needed to complete by week's end.

After several hours, the doctor entered the room. She sat in the chair next to me.

"Your dad is doing fine. He's still under the effects of the anesthesia and I have given him some pain medication. The cancer was outside of his prostate and on his bowel. I removed all that I could without damaging other organs. He will be much more comfortable when sitting after his incision heals."

"Good. Thank you." I hesitated. "What's next?" I expected her to say chemotherapy.

"I will see him for a follow-up appointment in a week or so. My secretary will call you with the date and time of the appointment. As far as an additional treatment, he may want to return to his regular oncologist for his recommendations, but he can make that decision after his follow-up with me."

She escorted me to Dad's bed, leaned toward him, and placed her hand on his shoulder. He was still groggy from the anesthesia. She relayed the information she had shared with me. He nodded turning his head and looking at me standing on the other side of his bed.

I reached for his hand. He blinked his eyes lethargically before forcing them open to stare at me.

"You come into the world in diapers, you go out in diapers." His words were mumbled and whispered as he grinned trying to make light of his condition, but I think it secretly bothered him.

Dad recovered quickly and was glad to be able to sit comfortably once again. His surgeon was pleased with his progress. He decided to return to his doctor, who advised no additional treatment other than continuing with the hormone therapy.

My summer break was coming to an end. Jasper was returning early to campus for soccer practice and joined us for dinner the night before. The four of us enjoyed grilled burgers with homemade potato salad, corn on the cob, and fresh fruit.

I went into the house to get the dessert and returned to see Jasper talking to Dad. They shook hands and stopped their conversation as I set the plate of cookies on the table.

With fireflies flickering in the yard like twinkling Christmas lights, we gathered around the fire pit for a campfire. It wasn't long before Dad excused himself and went to bed. My brother made himself scarce as well. I turned to Jasper.

"Hey, I have the ingredients for s'mores. Are you in the mood for one?"

"Sure, sounds like an excellent idea."

It was quiet inside the house as I entered. I assumed Dad was in bed and my brother in his room watching TV or playing video games. I petted Max on the head as I pass by him sleeping on the couch. Petey hopped down from a dining room chair and followed me to the kitchen. I gave him a kitty treat, grabbed one for Max, and quickly located the ingredients for s'mores and the roasting forks. Petey knew I had taken another treat from the bag. He trailed behind me and watched as I placed the treat before Max. I waited for him to eat it, because I knew if I walked away, Petey would have snatched it away from his sleepy companion.

Orange glowing sparks flew skyward as Jasper placed another log on the fire. I set the s'more ingredients on an empty chair, skewered marshmallows onto the end of the roasting forks, and handed one to Jasper before I sat in my chair. He sat in the chair next to me. Before long, our marshmallows were roasted, and we enjoyed the rather sticky sweet treat. I looked at the cloudless sky and stared at the stars. Jasper looked up.

"Are you searching for the constellations?"

"No, a satellite. If you look long enough, you can see one crossing the sky."

He reached for my hand, kissed the back of it, and looked skyward. He pointed to a star.

"Is that one?"

I looked to where he pointed.

"No, it's not moving."

He pointed again.

"How about that one?"

I laughed.

"Um, no."

He leaned toward me, held his hand skyward once again.

"How about this one?"

I looked to his hand. Something reflected the firelight. It was metallic, round, and…beautiful. I looked to his face. It was sincere, smiling. He rose from his chair and knelt on one knee.

"I know you don't want to get married for a while, but I would like you to know that my heart is committed to you. I love you and I hope you will do me the honor of becoming my wife…someday."

I looked from his face, tears welling in my eyes, and tried to focus through by blurred vision on the ring he held before me. I looked back to his face and smiled.

"Yes."

He rose to urge me to stand and slipped the ring on my finger before drawing me near. His lips touched mine before he brushed away the tears on my cheeks with his thumbs and cradled my face in his hands.

"Your dad is very excited about our engagement. Your brother, well, he is less emotional, but I think he is happy to have me as his brother-in-law."

"Dad knows?"

"Absolutely, out of respect, I asked for his blessing for your hand in marriage."

I extended my left hand and gazed at the ring.

"It's beautiful."

"I'm glad you like it."

He sat in a lounge chair and pulled me to his lap wrapping his arms around me as we laid back together.

"I love you." He whispered in my ear.

"I love you too." I snuggled next to him and laid my head on his shoulder. Content with the moment, we watched the fire until it was reduced to a pile of glowing embers before retiring for the evening.

We woke early the next morning and cooked a big celebratory breakfast for everyone.

"Something smells good." Dad ran his hand through his hair as he entered the kitchen.

I turned toward him.

"Yes, we are celebrating our engagement." I held my hand toward him so he could see my ring. He clasped my hand and turned it to the left and right scrutinizing each sparkle of the diamonds.

"That's wonderful. Beautiful ring. Congratulations." After a hug from Dad and Jasper receiving a handshake, my brother entered the kitchen as he overheard our conversation.

"Congrats to you both." He sat at the table and began putting food on his plate. Jasper and I looked at each other and smirked.

Our impromptu breakfast didn't last long. My brother was out the door after putting his plate in the dishwasher. Dad showered and left for work. Jasper helped clear the table. I knew he had an early afternoon soccer practice, so I pushed him out the door and finished washing the frying pan by myself. I would join him on campus in two weeks.

My Senior Year

With my car loaded, I drove back to college for my Senior year. I completed my summer classes, bringing me one step closer to earning my undergrad degree by Christmas. If Dad's health allowed, I hoped to enroll in classes and begin working toward my master's degree during the winter semester.

My life seemed like I was running on a gerbil wheel. Each year of college was like the previous one except the classes were more intense and demanding. This was Jasper's last year too. He continued to play on the soccer team, and I resumed my job in the library. I hoped to maintain my high grade point average while Dad's health weighed on my mind. He insisted I return to college. I prayed he would remain healthy until I came home in the spring.

My first week of college went smoothly. The oncologist ordered another scan for Dad to monitor the spread of his cancer. The doctor reviewed the results and recommended a round of chemotherapy. I planned to call my brother later in the evening to find out how the procedure went, but my phone rang as I got out of class.

"Hi."

"Hey, Dad is in pretty bad shape."

No 'hello' and I detected a tremor in his voice. I stopped walking.

"What's wrong?" I tried to remain calm as I stepped off the sidewalk onto the grass to allow other students to pass.

"We're still in the hospital. They gave him the first dose of chemo. They think he is having a bad reaction. It is difficult for him to breathe. It's crazy and scaring the hell out of me."

"What are they doing for him?"

"I'm not quite sure, but there is a whole team of doctors in there working on him."

"Do I need to come home?" I entered my dorm.

"You know Dad would want you to stay there. I'll call you later after I speak with the doctors. I just needed to talk to someone."

It troubled me knowing he was at the hospital alone.

"Do you need Grandma to be with you? I can call her and ask her to go to the hospital." I heard him sigh.

"No. I'm OK. I just needed to talk to you. I'll call you soon. Bye."

"Bye." I entered my room, picked up Petey, who greeted me at the door, and cuddled him close to my chest hoping to calm myself. Max looked at me from his curled position on my pillow.

I wanted to call Jasper, but I knew he was in class. He had practice afterward and would eat dinner with his team. I wouldn't see him until the evening.

I sat on the futon with Petey, staring at my phone that I set beside me, pleading for it to ring, and waited. The minutes ticked by lethargically as I petted my cat's silky fur. I sighed and crossed the room to get a bottle of water from the refrigerator when my phone rang. In a near run, I set Petey on the bed before picking up my phone.

"Well?"

"Oh, that was scary." My brother sighed.

"And?"

"They have everything under control now. He is resting and they plan to keep him overnight for observation."

"What happened?"

"They verified he had an allergic reaction to the chemo."

"My goodness."

"They plan to reduce the dose or perhaps try another combination of drugs when he returns for his next treatment."

"Good. Is he awake?"

"No, he's sleeping."

"Have him call me when he wakes."

"It may be better if he calls you after he is discharged and is home tomorrow."

"OK. Tell him I love him and call me if anything changes."

"Ok, I will, bye."

"Bye." I was shaking internally. Petey hopped from the bed, sat before me, and pawed at my leg. I picked him up and stroked his silky coat as I paced the room. Somehow, I knew I would not rest easy until I spoke to Dad.

* * *

As always, I have my phone on silent during class. Try as I might, I could not squelch the urge to check it often to see if I missed a call from Dad. I wanted to call him between classes but did not know if he had been released from the hospital, or worse yet, wake him while he was resting.

Unable to withstand the suspense any longer, I walked to the cafeteria for dinner and called him.

"Hi, honey."

"Hi, Dad. How are you feeling?"

"Better. That first dose of chemo was a little too much for my body to take."

His voice seemed shaky and weak.

"So, was it effective?"

"Too soon to tell."

"When is your next dose?"

"I have to call the doctor's office to see when he has scheduled it. He mentioned changing the medication, so I don't have another near-death reaction again."

"Good thinking. Are you home?"

"Yes, I came home just after noon. I've been sleeping most of the day."

"Good. Have you eaten anything?"

"Your brother made me a sandwich."

"He did? Please don't tell me it was peanut butter and jelly."

Dad chuckled.

"No, it was ham and cheese with mayo and a side of potato chips."

"Nice. I'm impressed. I hear the washing machine running, so I assume he is doing the laundry too."

"Yes, I just hope he doesn't put a red tee shirt in with the whites. I did that once. I ended up with pink underwear."

I smiled. It was comforting to know he still had a sense of humor.

"Well, get some rest, eat well, and hydrate. Love you, Dad. I'll talk to you soon."

"Love you too. Bye."

"Bye."

It was reassuring to know my brother had the situation well in hand. I assumed his high school teachers made accommodations for his time away from school to care for Dad and the completion of his assignments.

* * *

Dad underwent a second chemo treatment. After his third, he decided it would be his last. The side effects were too much for him to bear.

My heart seemed to shrink by his choice. I wanted him to fight, to survive, but I also wanted him to experience a quality of life for however long he had left to live. Even though I did not agree with his decision to stop treatment, I had no other choice than to respect his decision. After all, it was his choice to decide what was best for him.

The oncologist insisted Dad continue the hormone treatment even though I thought it was pointless to do so. He also proposed the option of a clinical trial. For the good of others and since Dad had no other options, he agreed to participate. He did not know if he was taking the experimental drug or a placebo. Since he experienced unpleasant side effects, he assumed he received the real thing. Dad opted out of the study within a week of beginning it.

* * *

The cats and I arrived home for the long Thanksgiving weekend. I entered the kitchen to find bottles of medications on the counter. I picked up one and read the label wondering what was being prescribed by his doctor.

Dad walked into the kitchen.

"I thought I heard your car pull into the driveway." He hugged me. I could feel his ribcage and his clothes hung on him like a scarecrow.

"Yes, the cats and I made it safely. I'm looking forward to a long, peaceful weekend and Thanksgiving dinner." I let Petey and Max out of the carrier and glanced over the kitchen. My brother managed to keep it tidy. "So, how are you feeling?"

Dad pulled out the nearest kitchen chair and sat like he was sinking into quicksand. His legs were weak.

"I'm doing my best." He glanced at his medications and nodded. "As you can see, the doctor keeps adding meds for me to take. I was diagnosed with a blood sugar condition, so one more was added for that as well."

* * *

I watched my husband from the corner of the room. He looked frail, weak. With the understanding his death was preordained, it seemed unfair to our children to have to watch us both die slowly. Maybe we knew our deaths would be early in our lives. In order to leave the physical world, we had to endure a lot of suffering to push us toward the acceptance of our fate.

"How much longer?" I looked at my spirit guide.

"Much depends on when he is ready to pass. A person's will and determination can be strong and allow them to stay for a longer time than planned. He may need encouragement to let go of this life and move onto the afterlife."

I looked at Elizabeth. She entered her life choosing us as her parents and understood subconsciously we would leave her at an early age. What did she need to learn? Independence? Self-reliance?

* * *

After watching Dad move lethargically from one room to the other, my brother and I dismantled the dining room table and relocated Dad's bed downstairs so he wouldn't have to climb the stairs to sleep every night.

While dusting the house, I discover paperwork in an open folder on Mom's desk outlining Dad's preparations for the end of his life. Like Mom, he worked with our priest to organize his funeral service, thoughtfully taking the burden off our shoulders.

We hosted the Thanksgiving dinner knowing it would be difficult for Dad to go to Grandma's house. I tried to remain upbeat and cheery, but in my heart, I knew it was the last time Dad would be sitting at the table for the holiday meal.

I was not in the mood to put up the Christmas tree, but I wanted to keep our lives as normal as possible. I brought up the boxes from the basement and went to work setting up the Christmas tree, ensuring it was secured to the windowsill. Dad rose from his chair and placed the angel on the top of the tree while I secretly snapped a picture with my phone. Over the next hour or so, I decorated the tree while Petey and Max explored and played, and Dad watched from his chair.

I stepped back to admire the tree before setting out the nativity and hanging up the stockings.

I prepared several meals, taped the cooking instructions on the aluminum foil, and placed them in the freezer for my brother to prepare later. The night before returning to campus, I called Jasper while I folded my laundry.

"Hey."

I had thought about this idea for the past month but wanted Jasper's opinion.

"Hi. I want to run something past you."

"OK."

"Since I technically have finished my bachelor's degree and you will be student teaching winter semester, I think it may be best to delay or take my master's classes online so I can stay home with Dad."

"What does he say about the idea?"

"I haven't told him yet."

Jasper was silent for a moment.

"Well, I think you should talk to your counselor once you get back to campus and ensure all of your undergrad credits are satisfied and get his advice before going forward."

"Good thinking. I'll do that."

I decided to leave Petey and Max home for the week and a half I would be away for exams. They would be good company for Dad while I was gone.

After explaining the situation to my counselor, he verified I had fulfilled my undergrad requirements and taking my dad's health into consideration, he advised I wait to take any additional classes. After finishing my exams, I packed up my room, checked out of the dorm, and drove home. As I drove, I was determined to put a smile on my face and make this Christmas a memorable one.

Petey and Max greeted me at the back door.

"The boys have been keeping me company and gave me little room on my pillow at night, but I'm no substitute for you." Dad remained seated in his favorite chair as I entered the living room.

I kissed Dad on his forehead before picking up Petey and Max and kissing the tops of their heads.

"Have they behaved?"

"Let's just say they have been entertaining. They certainly like to play." He closed his laptop, set it on the end table next to his chair, and noticed I was staring at it. "They are allowing me to work from home."

"That's nice. Are you hungry?" I knew it was close to lunchtime. Since my brother's car was absent, I assumed he was at school.

"Oh, I'm certain I could eat something. Surprise me."

I set the cats down, made a quick lunch for both of us, and joined Dad in the living room so I could visit with him while we ate. This was as good of a time as any to inform him of my decision.

"I completed my undergrad." I looked at Dad, hoping my next bit of news would meet his approval.

"Well done. Congratulations."

"So, since Jasper will not be at college next semester and after discussing the situation with my counselor, I am taking off next semester and will remain home with you. I can begin my master's degree online anytime, but my counselor has advised, and I agree, that I should wait to take classes for now."

"I see." He was quiet for a moment. "You can't sit around here waiting for me to die. Since we still own half of the partnership of Mom's company, perhaps you should begin taking over her job. I have been doing what I can while juggling my work responsibilities and doctor's appointments. I can begin orientating you as soon as you are ready."

I had thought to return to my old job, but his suggestion made more sense.

"Sounds good."

After unloading my car and putting everything away, I made a list of the Christmas cookies I wanted to make, took inventory of our baking supplies, and made another list of groceries needed before beginning dinner and starting my laundry.

A week before Christmas, I was in the kitchen baking the last Christmas cookie on my list. I noticed Dad made several trips to the bathroom. His face masked in agony as I stood in the doorway and he passed by me on his way to the living room.

"Are you OK?" I wiped my hands on a dishtowel as he sat in his favorite chair.

"I can't poop. I feel all backed up."

I called his oncologist, who advised I take him to the hospital.

"Your doctor wants you to go to the emergency room and have them see what the issue may be."

I helped him with his jacket, got him in the front seat of the car, and drove to the hospital. Pulling up to the front doors of the emergency room, I went inside and retrieved a wheelchair to get him inside.

UNTIL WE MEET AGAIN

We were fortunate the waiting room was empty. He was put on a bed in a secluded room and not in one divided by curtains. After x-rays and an examination, the doctor discovered a bowel blockage and determined Dad was too weak for surgery, so they were going to try to remove the blockage as gently as possible. I was asked to go to the waiting room while they performed a procedure.

I thought to call my brother, but the time on my phone indicated he was still at school. I distracted my mind by picking up the nearest magazine and paging through the advertisements trying to locate an article to read. I nearly bolted from my chair as I heard Dad's blood-curdling scream echo from the other room. My eyes welled with tears and the page before me blurred as I questioned how much longer he must suffer from his illness.

The doctor came out moments later.

"The blockage has been removed. His blood test indicates he has diabetes."

"Yes, it developed a little while ago."

"Has he taken his medication today?"

"I assume so. I mean, I don't monitor what he is taking every day."

"You may want to. His blood test indicates he either hasn't taken it or it needs to be adjusted. Please follow up with his doctor to ensure he is receiving the proper dose. I thought it would be a good idea for him to stay the night in the hospital for observation, but you Dad says he wants to go home."

As I expected.

* * *

As the holiday drew closer, our true and treasured gift for Christmas was simply being together. Grandma offered to shop for Dad, which he willingly gave her a list of the items he wanted for us. I placed my wrapped gifts under the tree and stared at the one with Dad's name on it. The thing it wished it contained was something I could not give him, time. Time to remain with us and to someday walk me down the aisle of the church on my wedding day. If Jasper and I were blessed with children, I wish he could be there to watch them grow, receive their hugs and kisses, hear their laughter, and listen to them explain their abstract artistic drawings.

Dad insisted on attending midnight Mass. We rented a wheelchair for him to use so he wouldn't exert himself too much. We spent Christmas day in our pajamas, enjoyed a big breakfast, opened our gifts, and took a lot of photographs. Grandma joined us in the early afternoon. We exchanged gifts with her, ate a nice dinner, and had my Christmas cookies for dessert. I had Grandma take a picture of the three of us with Petey and Max and promised myself to place it next to Mom's picture on my nightstand.

UNTIL WE MEET AGAIN

Jasper came to visit a few days later. We spent a quiet day at home putting together a puzzle. Dad seemed upbeat to have his future son-in-law to talk to but retired to his bed early in the evening, so we went to my bedroom to watch TV so he could sleep.

Jasper sighed before proposing his idea.

"I'm concerned about your dad. He doesn't seem to be doing very well."

"I agree. As much as I wish for his recovery, I know he has given up hope and reconciled with the end of his life. I found paperwork on Mom's desk describing the details of his funeral arrangements. In truth, I don't want to lose him, yet I don't want him to suffer any longer."

"So, hear me out. I'm not trying to sound pessimistic, but we don't know how much longer your father has to live. I know you don't want to get married for a while, but what if we do so after I finished next semester? Your father would be pleased to be present and to walk you down the aisle and it would give him something to look forward to as well. What do you think?"

I always dreamed of having a big wedding, but realistically, it would most likely only be immediate family, a few friends, and our kind neighbor. Having Dad walk me down the aisle was a must. I smiled.

"I would like him to be there too. So, yes, let's get married then."

"Let's pick a date." He took out his cell phone from his jean pocket and thumbed through the calendar until he came to the month of May.

We looked at the weekends. I didn't want to get married on a Sunday.

"How about the last Saturday of the month when the weather should be warmer?" I looked at Jasper seeking his approval.

"OK."

"And keep it small, immediate family and a few friends. I don't have much money in my bank account, but I want to pay for what I can."

"Maybe between the two of us, we can pay for the entire wedding. I assume you would want to have it at your church?"

I thought of Mom's flower garden. Her spring flowers would be in bloom then. I imagined being surrounded by floral colors representing her presence for the ceremony.

"I want to have our wedding in the flower garden. We can get someone to perform the ceremony by the arbor, set up enough chairs for everyone to sit, and there is a small aisle for Dad to walk the short distance to the opposite side of the garden."

"I like that idea."

"I doubt if we will be able to afford a honeymoon."

Jasper shrugged his shoulder.

"We can take one later."

I nodded.

"Besides, I would like to stay close to Dad to see him through to the end."

"I wouldn't have it any other way."

"We should rent an apartment after we are married, but it may not be a good idea to be bound to a lease for a year. Depending on how quickly Dad's health deteriorates, we may be spending most of our time here, if not living here, to care for him." I paused as Jasper nodded in agreement before continuing. "I guess we will see how he is feeling as we get closer to our wedding. We may be able to get away for a long weekend somewhere. As far as moving forward, I will meet with Mom's partner, gradually take over Dad's responsibilities with the company, and eventually move into her fulltime position. With Dad being ill, I think her partner has taken on most of the responsibility of her job. I would like to lighten the load from her. Dad is still working at his job even though I believe they have reduced his responsibilities there too. I'm not certain how much longer he can do so, but I think they understand that it gives him a purpose to keep living."

* * *

"I'm so proud of her. Elizabeth has always been a take-charge kind of person. It pleases me she will be married in the flower garden. I pray that her wedding day is sunny and pleasant."

My spirit guided nodded in agreement.

* * *

Jasper brushed a strand of hair away from my cheek and kissed my forehead. He sighed.

"Well, we have made enough decisions for now. We have time to figure out the rest over the next few months."

Making Arrangements

The next morning, Jasper and I shared our news as the four of us sat around the breakfast table. Dad reached for my hand and covered it with his palm.

"I think that is a wonderful idea."

He seemed to be doing well, considering his aggressive cancer was on a relentless quest to conquer his body. He continued to work from home. It helped to keep his mind off his illness. He informed Mom's partner I would be taking over for him and working part-time for now.

* * *

With the start of the new year, I kissed Dad on the forehead.

"I'll be back soon. If you need anything, call me."

He nodded his head as he sipped his coffee and shooed me away with a wave of his hand as he opened his laptop. I left and drove to the office to begin work.

It had been a long time since I set foot in the historic building. The familiar smell of polished wood greeted me as I listened to the creak of each oak stair as I ascended to the second floor. It was as if the building was sharing its memories of Mom's time spent within its walls, unfortunately, it was in a language I could not understand.

"Hello, Elizabeth." The secretary rose from her desk.

"Hello." I looked toward Mom's office.

"I understand you're going to be joining us." I followed her as she opened the door to Mom's office. "How is your Dad doing?" She allowed me to pass through the doorway before standing at the entrance.

"He's doing fine for now." I detected a scent of Mom's perfume lingering in the room as I stood in the center of the office. Scanning the desk and cadenza, the photographs were the same. Everything was the same. Dad hadn't changed a thing. I went behind the desk and picked up a framed copy of my favorite photograph, the one I had on my nightstand, of Mom and me. I was so little then. Maybe three years old. I went to return it but saw a white feather in its place. I picked it up, twirling it between my forefinger and thumb as I set the picture down, and turned toward the doorway as Mom's partner entered the room.

"Hello, Elizabeth. I'm glad you've decided to work here."

"Hi, thanks. I'm looking forward to it."

The phone rang in the reception area.

"Excuse me." The secretary dismissed herself.

I smiled at my new partner compelled to explain further.

"I plan to spend a few hours each day trying to orientate myself with the business. When I'm not in the office, I will be home having Dad continue to share what tribal knowledge he knows."

"How is your Dad?"

"He is holding his own for now."

"Good. Well, I'll let you get started. If you have any questions, feel free to ask."

I looked at the stack of printed reports on Mom's desk, ran my thumb through the corner's edge, and back to my partner.

"Thanks."

I looked at the feather in my hand. *Well, Mom, I'm going to give it my best. I'll admit, I'm a little overwhelmed and don't know where to begin.* I placed the feather beneath the protective glass of the desktop, sat in the chair, and exhaled.

* * *

I smiled with pride.

"She'll do just fine. It's a lot for her to absorb all at once. She just needs to take it a step at a time and ask questions when she doesn't understand something."

"*It is a lot of responsibility for one so young, but she will manage.*"

* * *

The following month was chaotic: taking Dad to the doctor, learning the operations of the business, planning my wedding, advising my brother through the end of his senior year of high school, and keeping the house in order. Dad's strength declined, mostly in his legs. It was difficult to watch his health deteriorate and accept the inevitable. My highlight of each day was talking to Jasper, my strength.

As I readied for work one morning, I entered the dining room to find Dad in tears as he lay in bed. He complained he was in pain. My brother had already left for school, so I called Grandma to help me get him into my car. I called his oncologist, who instructed me to take him to the emergency room. He would meet us there. After an x-ray was taken, the doctor concluded the cause of his pain was due to a growth on his spine that was pressing on a nerve. Dad was admitted to the hospital, pain medication was prescribed, and radiation treatments to the area was scheduled to reduce the size of the growth. He would come home once the growth had reduced in size and the pain alleviated.

* * *

I turned the calendar in my office to April before gathering what I needed to work from home. I was afraid to leave Dad alone. He had fallen a few times, so I purchased a cane to help him rise from his favorite chair and steady his balance as he walked to and from the bathroom. His medications increased and needed my monitoring to ensure he received the proper daily dose. I knew he wasn't eating like he should and assumed the fluid in his face was caused by the meds. When I asked the doctor, he confirmed my suspicion. He called the side effect a 'moon face.' Basically, his body was swelling up like a dry sponge placed in a bowl of water.

He sat in his favorite chair watching the noon news as I placed the TV tray in his lap hoping he would eat most of what I had prepared for lunch. On his tray was a tiny plastic cup containing his midday medication.

"It looks delicious." He sat up in his chair a bit taller, concern masking his face as he stared at me as I stood before him.

"Elizabeth, you look tired. This is getting to be too much for you. I think it is time we call Hospice."

Hospice? Was I a failure to him? I was doing my best.

"Is that what you want?"

"Yes, they can monitor my medication, help me shower, take me to the bathroom, and relieve some of the burdens from you. With them here, you can spend a few hours in the office every day and leave the house for errands without worrying about me."

Without knowing how much time Dad had left, I wanted to spend every moment with him and cast it to my memory. This was a decision of his choosing and I had to respect it.

"OK, I'll call them in the morning." I went to the kitchen before he could see my eyes welling with tears. I bit my trembling bottom lip and shed my tears before carrying my plate of salad to the coffee table and joining him for lunch.

Hospice was a godsend. They provided Dad with a walker to prevent him from falling and injuring himself. They also brought in a hospital bed and returned his bed to his bedroom. I was able to spend my mornings at work and join Dad for lunch during the week while a hospice nurse stayed with him. Our evenings were quiet, just the three of us eating dinner and tucking Dad safely into bed each night.

Jasper finished his student teaching and, with the insistence of his parents, walked commencement the first weekend in May. I decided not to participate since it would have been too much for Dad to be there.

UNTIL WE MEET AGAIN

A few weeks before our wedding, Jasper moved into our house to help with the preparations. He assisted Dad with his needs after the hospice nurse left after his morning shift. I often stand in the doorway of the kitchen and watch my future husband treat my father with such kindness and patience. I truly am marrying the right man.

For Better Or For Worse

The tent, table, and chairs were delivered the day before our wedding. Grandma arrived early the next morning to help organize and decorate. Jasper and I set up the table and chairs, added tablecloths, and our simple centerpieces. The arbor in the flower garden was framed by honeysuckle vines. We added white organza fabric and an additional bouquet at each corner to give it a romantic ambiance.

    I stood in the center circle of the flower garden among the chairs where our guests will be seated and turned in a slow circle. Mom's spring flowers were in full bloom. The vibrant colors, new mulch, potted plants, and decorated arbor was perfect. I smiled knowing Mom would be proud of my effort to keep her garden in order and have the ceremony within it.

Checking my phone, I had an hour before the ceremony. My elderly neighbor volunteered to oversee the food. I glanced at the tent as I passed by it on my way inside the house. She directed the caterer to the table where the buffet would be set out.

Mom's wedding dress, yellowed with age, and veil hung from the top of my closet door. I touched its delicate lace and recalled seeing her wedding photographs in an album. She was so beautiful on her wedding day. I preferred a different style of dress, but I was lucky this one fit me, and it was what I could afford. I'm certain Dad will be pleased when he sees me wearing it.

Grandma helped me slip on the dress. She pinned my hair into place while I did my make-up. She took the veil from the hanger, pushed the comb into my hair, and fluffed the material so the edges draped over each of my shoulders. With my bouquet of flowers in hand, I turned toward her.

Grandma smiled.

"You look lovely."

A rap sounded on my bedroom door.

"Elizabeth, it's time." My brother waited for me to appear.

Grandma opened the door to see him standing before the doorway dressed in his suit. She squeezed his arm as she passed by him and descended the staircase. He looked at me and smiled before presenting his elbow to escort me downstairs. He leaned toward me as we reached to top step.

"You look great."

I smiled.

"Thanks."

Dad waited at the bottom of the staircase. He straightened his suitcoat and ensured his tie was centered as he watched us descend.

"Oh, Elizabeth, you look so beautiful." He bit his bottom lip. "I wish your mother could see you now."

Blushing, I looked down at the carpeted floor before descending the final step and spied a white feather. I retrieved it and tucked it into my bouquet of flowers.

"I'm certain she is smiling down on us from above, Dad." I noticed his welling eyes. "Don't cry or I'll start crying." My brother unthreaded my arm from his.

We both dried our tears and pulled ourselves together as he offered his bent arm and I threaded mine through his. We took our time walking to the flower garden without Dad's walker to assist him. My brother followed closely behind him in case he should falter.

My eyebrows drew together at the angelic sound of a violin as we came around the side of the house and I spied the musician next to Jasper. I assumed he arranged the music as a surprise for our ceremony. Dad and I paused at the end of the short aisle as everyone stood.

UNTIL WE MEET AGAIN

* * *

"Oh, she looks lovely. Such a beautiful young woman."

"*You have every reason to be proud.*"

"I'm pleased she put the feather in her bouquet. It's as if I'm walking with them."

* * *

I glanced at Jasper, who looked away for a moment to compose himself to avoid crying. The priest waited before the arbor with my future husband to his left. Dad and I walked up the aisle passing our business partner and her family, my neighbor, Grandma, and Jasper's parents and grandparents. We stopped before the arbor, Dad kissed me on the cheek, placed my hand within Jasper's hand, and smiled at us both. My brother helped him to his seat before taking his place next to Jasper.

The music subsided. Our ceremony was short and sweet, just the way we wanted it. After the priest announced us as Mr. and Mrs. Jasper McLean, we walked down the aisle, received congratulations from our family, and posed for various wedding pictures. Jasper and I were first in line for food. Our meal was interrupted by clanking glassware encouraging us to kiss. The violinist played a song for our first dance as man and wife followed by the traditional father-daughter and mother-son dances. I didn't throw my bouquet, in truth, there was no one there to catch it. We cut our cake and served our guests, after which time Dad went to the house to rest.

At the conclusion of our reception, I changed out of my wedding dress. Everyone worked together to put away the leftover food and stack the tables and chairs for pick-up the next day.

Our first night as husband and wife was spent in a lovely room at a local hotel. With Dad needing care around the clock, as a family, we agreed it would be best for us to live with him and my brother. Dad insisted we move into his bedroom when we returned the next morning.

Come What May

My brother's high school graduation was a week later. Even if we pulled the car next to the sidewalk for Dad, the distance to the gym was too far for him to walk in his weakened condition. We requested a wheelchair from Hospice so he could attend the ceremony. I watched him clap as my brother crossed the stage, pride displayed on his face. It meant a lot to my brother too. He held his diploma over his head and nodded to Dad. Both were pleased they could share the milestone together.

With the help of Grandma, we had an open house for my brother the following weekend. I didn't want his accomplishment to be overshadowed by Dad's illness. He deserved the recognition for a job well done. Family, friends, and neighbors gathered to celebrate his achievement. At one point during the open house, I looked at my brother and caught him staring at me. He nodded and smiled silently thanking me for making his day memorable.

The following week, Jasper went with my brother to his college orientation. Thank goodness he chose an in-state university. He returned bubbling with excitement as he explained his classes, the tour of campus, and his tiny dorm room. We were confident he would adjust to campus life easily. I just prayed he didn't get caught up in the partying and stayed focused on his academics. I assumed I would have to give him the talk, a little sisterly advice before he left for school.

Petey was particularly persistent the next morning. I assumed he wanted his breakfast. He touched his paw to my face and kept circling my head. His tiny feet stepped on and pulled my hair and painfully pressed against the skin on my chest threatening to bruise it. I rose, slipped on my robe, and went downstairs to find Dad curled up like an infant on the floor. I knelt next to him.

"Oh, my god. Dad, what are you doing here?" I was unsuccessful in keeping my panic in check. I placed my palm on his head to see if he was running a fever. He was cold to the touch.

"I had to use the bathroom." His eyes remained closed.

Jasper hurried down the stairs dressed only in his underwear, looked at me with his mouth agape, and went to my side.

"Hey Dad, let's get you back into bed." He easily lifted his thin body in his arms and placed him on the sheets. I pulled the blankets over his chilled body.

"No more getting out of bed without calling us first." I scolded. I remembered a cowbell Mom's used to ring while watching my soccer games. Unfortunately, I didn't know if Dad had the strength to ring it, but I imagined he would be able to press the button on a desk bell like the one at the bookstore in town. I would see if I could purchase one today.

The three of us took turns sleeping on the couch at night and the hospice nurse visited twice each day. As Dad's pain increased, so did his medication. I tried to help Dad with his work but eventually called the office telling them he was no longer able to do so. They generously kept him on the payroll so he would continue to receive his health insurance. In my heart, I knew they wouldn't have to pay for his healthcare for much longer.

The second week in July, the hospice nurse met me at the back door as I arrived home from spending an hour at the office.

"Your Dad is transitioning. He should stop eating soon."

"Transitioning? What does that mean?"

"He is dying, and he has indicated to me that he wants to die at home."

I glanced toward the dining room before looking at the nurse again.

"How long does he have?"

"A few days, a week at most, but I'm not God, so that's just an estimate."

* * *

"It's sad. He will leave the children when they are so young." I paced the dining room glancing at the bed where my husband lay.

"*It is how he had planned before being born.*"

"Yes, I know. Nevertheless, to be so young and not have parents to guide them is not what I would have wished for them or any child."

"*It is also how they planned before they were born.*"

"A lesson they must learn." I looked at my spirit guide.

"*Yes.*"

* * *

Dad quit eating within a day. With one of us always by his bedside, we spoke of happier times and waited. He often mumbled incoherently and twitched his leg. I didn't know if the pain medication or lack thereof was causing him to do so. A hospice nurse was assigned to stay at the house day and night, monitor Dad's vitals, and care for his needs.

Dad stared at the corner of the room with the hint of a smile on his face late one afternoon. He was calm, peaceful. He turned his head toward me and lethargically blinked his eyes.

"Mom is here."

I tilted my head to the side wondering if I heard him correctly.

"She is?"

His hand quivered as he raised it from the sheet and pointed.

"She's there."

* * *

I turned to my spirit guide.

"He can see me?"

"Yes, the veil is being lifted from his physical world to our world. The time draws near. He will join you soon."

I looked at my husband and smiled. His suffering would soon end. He just needed to let go. I motioned for him to come toward me, encouraging him to join me.

* * *

"She looks beautiful. She is waving her hand for me to go with her."

I smelled the fragrance of Mom's perfume and looked to the corner of the room where he pointed but saw nothing. I looked back at Dad.

"Then maybe it is time for you to go and join her." I clasped his hand. "We'll be fine. You have taken care of every aspect, every detail to ensure we can carry on without you. It hurts me to see you suffer any longer. I love you and only want the best for you, Dad. Leaving us now and joining Mom is what is best."

"I love you too. I'm so proud of you and your brother. I'm proud of Jasper too. I couldn't have imagined anyone better for you to share your life." He sighed and closed his eyes as if keeping them open any longer drained his strength.

Max jumped onto the bed, curled next to Dad's side, and began to purr. I stroked his silky fur before placing Dad's hand upon the cat's neck where he could feel the vibration. Dad smiled slightly.

Not wanting to sound like an alarmist, I sent a text to Jasper and my brother. Within seconds, they appeared at Dad's bedside to say their final good-byes.

Shortly afterward, Dad slipped into a coma. We kept a vigilant watch knowing he would leave us soon. Max stayed by Dad's side as if waiting for him to cross over.

UNTIL WE MEET AGAIN

After a day of silence, Dad opened his eyes and looked at the three of us gathered around his bed. He looked at Max, moved his index finger several times stroking his fur.

"I want to say good-bye before I go. Mom is waiting for me and I think it is time I joined her."

I kissed his cheek.

"Good-bye, Dad. We love you. Tell Mom we love and miss her."

"Bye, Dad. Love you. Love to Mom too." My brother squeezed his hand gently in a final handshake before reaching for my hand across the bed and we clasped hands.

"Bluebirds. I have always liked bluebirds." The corners of his mouth turned upward as he nodded his head slightly before closing his eyes. Within minutes he took his last breath.

Max hopped down from the bad as the nurse came forward, grasped his wrist, listened to his heart with his stethoscope, and shook his head indicating Dad had passed. He left the room to call Hospice, file the report, and make the necessary arrangements.

Petey tapped the side of my leg. I picked him up, placed him in my lap, and stroked his fur as the three of us sat around the bed in silence, a little stunned Dad's suffering was finally over.

* * *

I watched as his soul rose from his body and he stood on the floor. He looked back to the vessel that had once contained it and our loved ones consoling themselves over their loss.

"Hello dear." I greeted.

He turned to look in the corner of the room where I stood with my spirit guide close by.

"Hi." He came and stood before me. "You waited for me."

"Along with others." I motioned to my spirit guide. "He has been with me always, and so has yours." I looked to the opposite corner of the room near the ceiling where my husband's spirit guide hovered.

My husband turned toward the corner. He watched as his spirit guide descended, stood before him, and nodded his head once.

My husband returned his nod.

"Thank you for watching over me." He looked back at me. "Now what do we do?"

"You have three days before you must cross over. You may spend it visiting family, friends, your favorite places, however, you chose."

"What happens once I cross over?"

I looked to my spirit guide and glanced at my husband's spirit guide.

"You'll find out when you get there." I smiled. "Since your three days begins now, what would you like to do?"

UNTIL WE MEET AGAIN

He looked back to our children and Jasper.
"I would like to stay with them for a while."

* * *

The hospice nurse went to the kitchen and gathered all of Dad's medications in a plastic bag and waited for the funeral home personnel to arrive.

The three of us remained with Dad and spoke of fond memories. Even though he was no longer with us, we said our final good-byes before he was taken away. It was peaceful and bonding and our first step in healing the loss of our patriarch.

Within an hour, two men from the funeral home picked up Dad's body. I went to his bedroom closet to retrieve the garment bag containing his burial clothes. Bending down to pick up his pair of black dress shoes, I discovered two white feathers lying together on the floor. *They're together.* Knowing the men were waiting downstairs, I placed the feathers on the nightstand before leaving the bedroom and giving the men Dad's clothing.

The next day, Hospice collected the equipment they had brought to the house. I watched the men take the bed, the last place Dad laid his head, from the dining room. Jasper and my brother set up the dining room table. It was strange to pass by it and not have the hospital bed there any longer. I called Dad's lawyer to set his affairs in motion.

Sighing, with my coffee cup in hand, I walked through the quiet house one morning glancing at family photos on the walls, tables, and shelves. My life, our family paradigm, now changed and my responsibilities increased once again.

Putting Dad To Rest

On the day of Dad's funeral, we shouldered the surreal experience of putting our remaining parent to rest. We stood in the back of the church for the service to begin. Dad was less active in the community than Mom. There were empty pews toward the back of the church, but among the guests were his boss and coworkers.

Most of the details for the funeral were outlined in the paperwork. We honored Dad's requests and agreed collectively on options he overlooked. I stared at the flowerless altar as my brother, Grandma, Jasper, and I took our place in the front row for the service to begin. Even though flowers were an expression of sympathy and respect, Dad preferred a donation to a charity of his choice.

The priest droned on. I wasn't listening. I noticed Grandma's hand raised toward her face. She was usually steadfast, strong. I could only imagine what she was going through as she dabbed a tissue at each corner of her eye. It was unnatural to lose a daughter and now a son-in-law. Maybe their deaths were harder on her than it was on us. I admired her unwavering faith, her belief in life after death, and was thankful she remained by our side to see us through the emotional day.

As the Mass ended, I closed my eyes and bowed my head for the priest's blessing. A picture formed within my mind of Jesus cupping his hands above my head as if blessing me himself. I opened my eyes and raised my head. Did I imagine it or was it a message?

We followed the casket out of the church and stood watching as it was loaded into the hearse. An incessant chirping drew my attention. I turned to look at the hood of a nearby car to see a bluebird jumping up and down. I knew Dad was fine. We got into the car and drove to the cemetery. I stared at the family tombstone as I sat next to the grave and the priest began to speak. Dad's name and lifespan dates would be added to the marker. I watched as they lowered his casket into the ground where his body would lay in rest next to his beloved wife throughout eternity, together again.

UNTIL WE MEET AGAIN

The luncheon lasted a few hours with guests sharing memories of my parents. As the hall emptied, Grandma and I helped the volunteers tidy up. She glanced at me.

"Well, I think it was a nice send-off, don't you?" She set several small serving dishes on a tray. I placed the two bowls in my hands on the tray too.

"I think it was lovely. Thank you for overseeing the food. It was delicious as always."

She smiled as she picked up the tray from the buffet table and went to the kitchen.

Jasper's arm draped over my shoulder. He hugged me toward him and kissed my forehead. My brother stood before me brushing the palms of his hands together.

"All of the tables and chairs are put away. Is there anything else we need to do?"

I looked around the hall. The custodian would take care of the floor, not that it looked dirty, but it could use a good mopping.

"Let me check with Grandma."

I went into the kitchen. The volunteers were washing the dishes and counters. I searched for her among the women and spotted her near the large commercial refrigerator.

"Grandma, is there anything else we can do before we leave?"

She looked about the room.

"No, why don't you go home? It's been a long day. I'll call you later."

"OK Thank you for your help today." I hugged her.

"Oh, anytime."

Going Forward

I laid Dad's neckties neatly on our bed to display their patterns. After my brother and Jasper picked out a few they wanted to keep, I didn't have the heart to part with what remained, especially the ones I gave him for Father's Day or other holidays. Since home economics was no longer offered at my high school when I attended, I didn't know how to sew, but I assume Grandma would be able to help me as an idea came to mind. I called her on my cellphone.

"Hello, you."

"Hi, Grandma. Do you know how to sew?"

"Yes, don't you recall the baby blankets I quilted for you? Well, that was long ago, and you were an infant, so probably not. Knowing your mom, I imagine she packed them away somewhere."

"My business partner thought it would be a good idea to take a week off. I have been going through Dad's clothing and donating it. I want to do something special with his neckties though. I thought it would be nice to make pillows and a throw, or two if there are enough ties. It would be nice for my brother and me to have a nice keepsake. What do you think?"

"I think that is an excellent idea. Bring them over and we'll see what we can do with them."

I folded the ties and placed them in a cardboard box, descended the stairs, and entered the kitchen to find Jasper on his laptop.

"What are you doing?" I set the box on the table, leaned toward him, and kissed his cheek before looking over his shoulder at the screen.

"Applying for a job at the high school." He turned toward me wrapping his arm around my waist and pulling me near him. He glanced into the box. "What are you up to?"

"I'm going to Grandma's. She has agreed to help me make something with Dad's ties.

"His ties?" His eyebrows drew together.

"Yes, like a throw or pillow. I'm certain Grandma will come up with something useful."

"OK. I'll be here when you get back." He kissed me and patted my butt before releasing me.

The drive to Grandma's took only a few minutes since she lived just on the other side of town. I knocked on her door and heard her voice echoing from inside the house.

"Come on it."

With the box of ties in hand, I entered her kitchen.

"Hi, Grandma." I set the box on her table next to her sewing basket.

"So, let's see what you have here." She began pulling Dad's ties one by one from the box and inspecting them. "My, he has a lot of ties."

"I couldn't part with them and thought it would be nice to make something out of them."

"Well, from what I can see, many have spots on them from food or coffee. They need to be washed."

"Don't they need to be dry cleaned?"

"No, we can put them in the washing machine on the gentle cycle and set the water to cold." She stared at the ties imagining the possibility of my idea. "I think you can easily make two pillows and a throw, maybe even two throws."

"Sounds good to me. How do we get started?"

She opened her sewing basket, selected two hook-like things, and handed me one.

"These are seam rippers. We can take the ties apart while we visit and watch TV."

My eyebrows raised, questioning if I heard her correctly.

"Take them apart?" I did not like the idea of ruining something that belonged to Dad.

"I know it seems destructive, but the interior of the ties needs to be removed and the exterior washed and pressed to make them easier to work with."

We each took an armload of ties to the couch and placed them between us. Grandma turned on the TV before showing me how to disassemble a tie. She thought we should also save the underside of each monocolored end even though the material lacked a pattern. It took a long time to take each tie apart. I discovered my average was three dismantled ties per hour.

With the start of another TV program, I check my phone for the time. It read five o'clock. I looked at the piles we had accumulated. One for the exterior and interfacings, and a discard pile for the off-while inside material and various colored crinkled threads. I sighed as I added the pieces of the dismantled tie to their appropriate piles.

"Well, I need to get home and get dinner ready. We were able to get some of it done at least."

Grandma adjusted her glasses on the bridge of her nose to help her locate a black thread on one of Dad's dark blue ties. She hooked the seam ripper under the stitch and pulled.

"I can continue to work on what is left this evening and wash what we have done this evening."

Eager to complete the project before returning to work, I knew my schedule was free of commitments the remainder of the week but was not certain if Grandma was available.

"Do you have anything planned tomorrow?"

"No, so you can come over anytime. Just give me a call and let me know you are on your way."

"I will."

Grandma set aside the tie she was taking apart and walked me to the door.

"See you tomorrow."

"Probably in the morning. I'll bring lunch for us. Bye, Grandma."

* * *

When I arrived at Grandma's house the next morning, she had a laundered pile of tie parts on the kitchen table with her ironing board and iron set up next to it.

"I thought you could start ironing and I will finish taking apart the last of the ties. There are only a few more to do."

The pile of ties on the couch looked like more than a few to me. I looked at the iron knowing I had used one only a few times in my life. Grandma must have assumed so too as she picked it up to choose the settings.

"Since most of the ties are silk, we will have to keep the temperature low." She turned the small dial. "There. Wait a minute or two for it to warm up." I handed her the containers of chicken salad and fresh strawberries. She went to the kitchen and set our lunch inside. "Do you want anything to drink?"

"No, thank you. Maybe later."

She filled a glass with water she kept chilled in the refrigerator and took a long sip before returning to me. Selecting one of the washed ties, she placed it on the ironing board.

"It may be best to put the right side down and then run the iron over the cloth. If the iron sticks to the cloth, then it is too hot." She turned the tie over to the other side, pressed it, picked it up, and hung it over the back of her kitchen chair. "You work on this pile and I'll keep dismantling."

I imitated her demonstration while she sat on the couch, turned on the TV, and selected a tie from what remained.

After working several hours, we stopped to enjoy our lunch. Grandma took four chocolate chip cookies from the freezer and popped them into the microwave to warm them. Her cookies were better than mine or maybe they just tasted better because I didn't make them.

Resuming our responsibilities, I finished ironing the colorful ties and moved onto the smaller interface pieces. Grandma finished taking apart the last tie. She carried the pile of pieces to the washing machine and started it. She watched as I continued to iron, lost in thought.

"You will have to decide what size pillow and throw you want to make."

UNTIL WE MEET AGAIN

I had no idea what size they should be.

"What size do you think the pillows should be?"

"Most decorative pillows are fourteen or sixteen inches. The size you make may be determined by which size pillow inserts we find at the store. We will also have to purchase muslin for the backing. A throw is about half the size of a blanket." The washing machine swished in the background as she grew impatient at being idle. "We can't do much more today. Shall we go shopping tomorrow morning and see what we can find?"

"Sure. Let's eat out for breakfast. I'll come by and pick you up at eight o'clock."

"Sounds good. Here, let me finish ironing. I'll see you bright and early tomorrow morning."

* * *

I pulled into Grandma's driveway at eight o'clock in the morning. As expected, I hardly put the car in park before she stood by the passenger's side door. Always prompt and eager.

We enjoyed a pleasant breakfast at the local diner before going to the store to find a wide selection of pillow inserts. Once deciding on the fourteen-inch size, we purchased the necessary supplies and returned to her house.

We washed, dried, and ironed the muslin. Grandma found some tissue paper and we measured and cut a fifteen-inch square pattern for the pillows and a thirteen-inch square pattern for the throw, both allowing for a half-inch seam allowance.

We placed the ties on the backs of the kitchen chairs in groups of like colors. Grandma stepped back to view the organized ties.

"What color pillow would you like?"

I scanned the various options, uncertain which one to select. I liked the ties in the shades of brown, but I also liked the idea of having a pillow made from Dad's Christmas ties to place in his chair for December.

"Do you think it would be too selfish of me to want two?"

"I think that is perfectly fine. What do you have in mind?"

"I thought it would be nice to have one in browns and beiges to match the couch and one made of Dad's Christmas ties to place in his chair during the holiday."

Grandma smiled.

"I think that's a lovely idea. You will have to call your brother to find out his preference."

Under Grandma's tutelage, we selected several shades of brown and beige ties and placed them diagonally face down on a square of muslin. Ensuring the entire square was covered, we pinned the edges of the ties together, stitched them on her sewing machine, and pressed the seams open before placing it on the muslin square with the right side face up. I sewed over the seams to attach it to the muslin square and trimmed the excess material that exceeded the edge. Grandma held it up to inspect it.

"Well, there's one." She placed it on the table. "On to the next."

I sent a text to my brother before beginning the next square. Grandma set aside the Christmas ties as she sorted through the piles. Within seconds my phone chimed. I read the text aloud.

"I don't care." As I assumed. I finished pinning, sewing, and trimming the second square.

After completing both sides of my pillow, Grandma showed me how to add the zipper, finish the seams, and put the insert inside. I examined my work. *Not bad for an amateur.*

Grandma placed another pair of muslin squares before me.

"What does your brother prefer?"

"He said he didn't care. Maybe we should just choose a color that we have the most of and see how it looks, but nothing too wild though."

At the end of the week, Grandma and I were able to complete the throw and all three pillows. We displayed them on her couch, stepped back, and admired our accomplishment. I looked at Grandma.

"Thanks for your help. I wouldn't have been able to do this without you."

"There are plenty of church women who could have helped you. I'm glad it was me though." She looked at me and smiled.

"Me too."

Empty Nesters

"Do you have everything?" I stood on the edge of the driveway watching my brother throw his duffle bag of clothes into the trunk of his car.

"If I don't, you can either send it to me in the mail or I can come home and get it. I'm not that far away, you know." He slammed the trunk shut.

"I know. Call me when you get to college."

"You sound like Mom." He stood before me. "I'll be fine, and I promise to call you when I arrive if I don't forget." He smirked as he hugged me before turning to Jasper.

"Take care of her." He grasped my husband's hand.

"You know I will."

Jasper and I watched as he backed the car out of the driveway, waved as he honked the horn, and drove away.

* * *

The house was quiet as I rose for work the next morning. I made coffee while Petey wove between my legs reminding me his stomach was empty. Max sat in the kitchen doorway watching his fur brother degrade himself.

As I opened a can of cat food and divided it between the cats, the sound of running water from above indicated Jasper was in the bathroom. He had an interview at the administration building for a teaching and coaching position at the high school. I sipped my coffee while buttering the golden-brown toast.

While I nibbled on my simple breakfast, I packed my lunch for work.

"Good morning, beautiful." Jasper kissed my cheek before helping himself to a cup of coffee and a slice of toast, which he smothered with strawberry jam.

"Good morning." I smiled before scanning his black suit. "You look nice. All set for your interview."

"As ready as I will ever be."

I reached to straighten the collar of his shirt.

"You'll do fine. What time is your interview?"

Jasper looked at the clock on the microwave.

UNTIL WE MEET AGAIN

"In twenty minutes. I better be on my way." He kissed me and headed toward the door.

"Bye. Good luck." I patted Max on the head before going to our bedroom to get ready for work. Petey trailed behind me.

Showered and dressed, I drove the short distance into town while squinting my eyes from the strobe-like effect of the sun illuminating the leaves of the trees and projecting their shadows onto my windshield. I should have walked to work on such a beautiful day, but I would have arrived late for our morning meeting.

I greeted our secretary as I passed by her desk and opened the door to my office. It hadn't changed much since it became mine. I added a few pictures of Jasper and me together and Petey and Max captured in cute poses.

The meeting was detailed and lengthy with sales projections, marketing, and product inventory updates. My brain was mush after trying to absorb the information presented. I sighed as the meeting was adjourned.

I looked out my office window as I entered. The sunshine looked inviting. I grabbed my lunch and cellphone, left the building, and walked past the quaint shops while glancing in their windows. The streetscape looked lovely with its beautiful hanging baskets filled with pink everblooming petunias on the lampposts. I passed the candy store. *Ah, surprise bags.* The bookstore. *I should start reading again.* It's been a while since I have read something for pleasure. I entered the park, passed the gazebo, and sat on a bench facing the river. With the sound of the waterfall over the dam in the background, I opened my lunch and unwrapped my sandwich.

A group of boys were fishing on the river to my right and a couple sat on the other side of the river at a picnic table sharing a pizza. I looked at the gazebo as I took a bite of my sandwich. The city rented it out for weddings. I had imagined my wedding ceremony being there too. I smiled. My wedding was perfect, and I would not have wanted it any other way.

A motion to my left drew my attention. I looked at the water flowing over the dam to see a man standing on its crest. I stopped chewing. Did he realize how dangerous it is to walk along the top of the dam? The cement was slimy and slippery, and he could fall. Couldn't he read the posted warning signs? I looked closer at the man's face. *Dad*?

He smiled, dressed in his funeral suit. He nodded his head and waved. A calmness came over me. I smiled, blinked my eyes, and he was gone.

My smile faded as I scanned the length of the dam and the surrounding area, but he was nowhere in sight. I sighed, a little deflated. I ate another bite of my sandwich and chewed slowly as I thought. I saw him, didn't I? Did he just stop by to say hello? Did he want me to know he was fine?

Throughout the remainder of my lunch break, I continued to glance at the spot where Dad had stood, questions flooding my mind. With one last look at the waterfall, I packed up my lunch bag and walked back to the office.

I stared at the emails displayed on my laptop. Unable to concentrate, I sent a text to my brother to see how he was doing. Assuming he may be in class, I set my phone aside and forced myself to open an email. My phone chimed.

"I'm doing fine. Keeping up with classwork and meeting lots of people. Will call you later."

I sent a thumbs-up emoji and redirected my attention to the email.

The afternoon dragged on and on. I was eager to know the results of Jasper's interview. I thought to call him but wanted to watch his facial expressions and his body language while he explained his response to posed questions.

I entered the kitchen after work and inhaled the aroma of something deliciously prepared for dinner. Jasper closed the oven door and looked at me.

"How was your day?" He smiled as he uncorked a bottle of wine, poured a glass, and handed it to me.

"Fine. What's all this?" I glanced about the kitchen wondering why the table was not set.

"I thought I would treat you to dinner. If you will allow me to escort you to your table, my lady." With the bottle of wine in his hand, he presented his arm with his elbow bent.

I couldn't help but grin as I threaded my arm through his and he led me to the flower garden where the cast iron white table was set for dinner for two, flowers, and a flickering candle. He held my chair as I sat and guided it forward. He removed a plate covered by a glass dome to reveal cheese with crackers. I looked at him.

"You really put a lot into this."

He smiled and raised his eyebrows several times teasingly.

"Nothing but the best for you, my dear."

"Is this a celebratory dinner?" I assumed he may have gotten the teaching position.

"A celebration of us." He leaned down and kissed me before sitting across from me and pouring himself a glass of wine.

I opened my mouth to speak. Jasper anticipated my question.

"The interview went well. I was told they have several candidates and I will be notified tomorrow if I have made it to the second round."

I sipped my wine before setting my glass on the table.

"Second round?"

"Yes, if I make it to the second interview, I have to prepare a lesson plan and present it to a panel."

"A panel? How many interviewed you today?"

"Four. The principal, assistant principal, department head for social studies, and another teacher. I assume the teacher taught social studies."

I raised my glass.

"Here's to you moving onto round two." We clinked our glasses, nibbled on cheese and crackers, and I shared my experience at the park while we waited for our dinner to cook.

"So, what do you think?" I wanted Jasper's opinion of my sighting of Dad.

"Did he look well?"

"Yes, and a little younger too. He appeared happy."

"Well, maybe that's what he wanted you to know. That he is happy." Jasper checked the time on his phone. "Be back in a second."

I sipped my wine and waited. Jasper emerged from the house carrying two plates. He placed one before me. It contained lasagna, green beans, and salad with a breadstick on the side of the plate.

"It looks delicious." I waited for him to sit before I began to cut into the pasta with the side of my fork. The lasagna melted in my mouth causing me to close my eyes and savor its flavor. It was one of my favorite comfort foods. "Very good."

"Thanks."

Since Dad was gone and my brother was away at college, I wanted to begin classes toward my master's degree. However, I could not justify the expense since the degree did little for my advancement in the family partnership. I assumed Jasper would need to complete his master's degree for his career in teaching. I set my fork on my plate and reached for my glass of wine.

"From what I understand, you will want to get your master's degree to receive larger raises at work. Or at least, I believe that is how the field of education works."

"Yes, but I have to get the job first."

"Either way, you are still going to be a teacher, so earning your master's degree is a must."

"True. What about you?" Jasper shoveled the forkful of green beans into his mouth.

"I have always wanted to achieve a master's in marketing/business. It's a goal I had, but I'm having difficulty justifying the expense."

"Well, if you want to get your degree, I think you should get it."

"I used to think I would be working somewhere else, like another city, in another company. Through the turn of events, my career has been steered toward our family partnership. I feel the degree is no longer necessary."

He rose from his chair as he finished eating.

"Ready for dessert?"

* * *

I was at work the next day when my cell rang. It was Jasper.

"Hey."

"Hi, I got a call for a second interview."

I could tell he was smiling on the other end of the line.

"Nice. Congrats. What lesson are you going to present?'

"I went over some of the lessons I presented during my student teaching. I chose one on the Civil War."

"Ah, a subject you know well. When is your presentation?"

"On Monday. With school beginning in two weeks, they must fill the position quickly or hire a sub to cover the staff opening until they do. Anyway, it gives me the weekend to prepare."

Sunday afternoon, Jasper called me into the dining room. He motioned for me to sit at one end of the table while he took his place at the opposite end where his laptop was open.

"I want to run through this lesson, see what you think."

"OK." I sat and clasped my hands in my lap.

"I need you to begin the stopwatch on your phone when I start talking. I have to stay within the thirty to thirty-five-minute time limit, no more, no less."

I took my phone from my back pocket of my shorts and nodded for Jasper to begin.

"Good morning. The lesson I am presenting today is about…"

I pressed the button to start the time and focused my attention on my husband. The topic was interesting. Jasper was a natural. Confident. Charismatic. Knowledgeable. I pressed stop at the end of his lecture and asked a few questions as if I was a student. I glanced at my phone.

"You stayed within the time they are allotting you. I thought it was good. You even told me a few things I didn't know."

Jasper exhaled relieving some of his nervousness.

"Good."

* * *

Jasper's presentation went well, or at least he thought it did.

"They will call me once they have reached a decision. Until then, I plan to look for other available teaching jobs in the area in case I don't get this one." He kept his phone by his side, waiting eagerly for it to ring.

In the evening of the third day after his presentation, he received a phone call from the principal asking him to come into the high school. He dressed in his suit the next morning and went as requested.

Since I had not received a call from him throughout the day while I was at work, it could either mean one of two outcomes. One, he didn't get the job. Or two, he got the job but wanted to tell me in person.

I arrived home after work to find the house empty, well, except for Petey and Max greeting me at the back door as usual. I called Jasper.

"Hi." He sounded tired.

"Hi. Where are you?"

"In my classroom."

"You got the job?" I was certain he detected the excitement in my voice.

"Yes, and very little time to prepare lesson plans. I'm leaving now and will fill you in on the details when I get home. Love you, bye."

I made a quick dinner of BLT sandwiches and chips. Jasper explained his acceptance of his new job, filling out paperwork, his assigned classes, the lists of students, materials, and his classroom. He was also offered the position as the head coach for the boys' and girls' soccer teams, which he accepted.

After a three-day holiday weekend, Jasper reported for his first day of work as a teacher. His hours were long since afterschool soccer practice and games added to his schedule.

On the morning of the first day of Autumn, Jasper left for school before I rose from bed for work. My stomach was upset, a little queasy. *Not the flu.* With Petey and Max in tow, I went to the kitchen and fed them before pouring cereal into a bowl and dousing it with cold milk hoping my stomach would settle once there was something in it. My eyes closed as I savored the first bite. I finished the contents of the bowl, set it in the sink, and ran to the bathroom. I leaned over the toilet as my breakfast splashed into the water. It didn't stay in my stomach very long. The milk was still cold as I threw it up.

An Unexpected Change

I suffered from flu-like conditions for a week and a half. Strange, I did not run a fever. Unable to cope with it any longer, I scheduled an appointment during lunch with my doctor. She did a routine physical and entered the examining room with the results.

"Elizabeth, you are pregnant."

My mouth dropped open. It was the last thing I expected her to say. Had I missed a period? Maybe I miscounted the weeks. The doctor continued.

"I assume this is unexpected."

"Yes."

"I consider pregnancy a blessing. Once you get over the shock, perhaps you will too. The nausea should subside by the end of the first trimester. Here are some prenatal vitamins you need to begin taking daily. Do you have any questions?" She handed me a large white plastic bottle.

"My due date?"

"The baby can arrive before or after the due date by as much as a week or so. But your due date is June 12th."

"June."

"If you have any questions, call me. Stop at the front desk to schedule your next monthly appointment." She handed me the checkout paperwork. "They will have a packet of information for you to read through as well."

"Thanks."

I sat on the examining table for a moment.

"A baby?" Was I ready for a baby? Not that I had any choice now. I mean, I want children, someday. I thought of my responsibilities at work. I was finally feeling settled and confident. I would have to take time off for doctor appointments. How much time would I be away from the office after the baby arrives? Oh, how would Jasper feel about becoming a father? I knew he liked children, but to be burdened with one of his own when he was just starting his job teaching, coaching, and working toward his master's degree. At least my due date was in June after school was dismissed for the summer. Jasper would be home to help with the baby. I smiled. When and how do I tell my husband that he is going to be a daddy?

I returned to the office and finished a pile of invoices before leaving early and going to the store. I found a card with a photograph of what I assumed was a husband and wife holding the hands of a child walking down a sidewalk. I opened it. It was blank inside. Perfect. I grabbed a gift bag and I went to the baby department hoping to find something gender-neutral. As luck would have it, I discovered a yellow onesie with the perfect message on the front.

I checked my phone for the time. Jasper would arrive home soon, so I rushed into the pizza shop and picked up dinner, put the onesie into a gift bag, and wrote a note on the inside of the card. The table was set with the present on his plate as he entered the kitchen.

"How are you feeling?" He kissed me before setting his duffle bag on the floor in the dining room.

"The same." I carried two glasses of ice water to the table and set them down before I sat.

Jasper pulled his chair out to sit and looked to his plate. "What's this?"

I tried to curtail my smile.

"A big surprise." My heart was pounding so rapidly I could hardly breathe. "Open the card first."

Jasper's eyebrows drew together as he grinned at the photograph on the front. He opened the card and read it aloud.

"The only thing better than having you as my husband will be our baby having you as a Dad." His mouth fell open as he stared at me. "You're pregnant?"

Tears welled in my eyes.

"Yes."

Jasper jumped out of his chair screaming with joy. He clasped my hand encouraging me to stand from my chair and kissed me before pulling me into his arms and embracing me in his arms. It was at that moment he began to cry, as did I.

After I wiped away my tears, I looked at his smiling face.

"I assume you are happy about this?"

"Over the moon. When are you due?"

"June 12th, right after your school year ends."

"Well, I couldn't have timed that any more perfectly, could I have?"

I laughed. Typical male taking all of the credit.

"Open the rest of your present."

We returned to our seats and he pulled out the onesie from the bag.

"I love Daddy." He looked at me. "Aw, it is perfect. Thank you." He leaned over and kissed me again.

* * *

I held my granddaughter in my arms. Her precious, chubby face conveyed contentment. She had chosen well, for I knew her parents would embrace her with all their hearts, give her a good home, and ensure her needs were met. She is lucky in that way and I am thankful.

I brought her fisted hand to my lips and kissed it.

"Time to go little one. Your parents are waiting. They will revel in every kick and summersault they will feel within your mother's body, they will guide you through life teaching you right from wrong, they will be there to celebrate your successes and pick you up and support you when you fail. Above all, they will love you as I do. Until we meet again." I kissed her on her forehead and placed her in the arms of her spirit guide. She opened her blue eyes, smiled, and reached her hand toward me.

"Enjoy your life and know that I love you." Looking over my shoulder, I posed a question. "When will she become one with her body?"

"*Times vary. However, many choose when the heart begins to beat.*"

I looked at my daughter and her husband. They were happy. I was happy for them too.

* * *

Jasper helped himself to another slice of pizza.

"A daddy. Wow."

"You're excited?"

"Beyond excited. I can't wait for him to get here."

"Or her to get here."

Jasper clasped my hand and brought it to his lips.

"Or her." He kissed the back of my hand. His eyebrows raised. "Are we going to find out the gender before he or she is born?"

"I think we can find out when they do an ultrasound at around twenty weeks, but I want to have a baby reveal party to announce the gender. Then we can decorate the nursery for whichever it is."

"Do you have a preference? A boy or a girl?" He bit into his slice of pizza.

"Not really? What about you?"

He chewed as he tilted his head to the side and thought.

"Either will be a blessing." He grabbed his glass of water. "June seems like a long way away." He took a drink.

"With work, coaching, and your classes, it will go by quickly."

Jasper paused as he reached for another piece of pizza.

"When do you want to tell everyone we are expecting?"

Even though I was excited to share the news with my brother, grandma, my in-laws, and people at work, I was hesitant.

"I think it would nice to keep our good news between the two of us until I begin to show. It can be our little secret. Maybe we can do it at Thanksgiving or Christmas when everyone will be together. We can host dinner and tell everyone then. What do you think?"

He smiled.

"I like the idea of keeping it a secret, our secret, until then."

* * *

Between the morning sickness and work, my energy level was quite low anyway. I slept more than usual too. Afternoon naps on the weekends became a needed rest time. My prenatal appointments went smoothly, and the baby was developing at a normal rate.

Thanksgiving was a week away. I couldn't fasten my pants comfortably. I went to work with them unfastened at the waist. During lunch, I visited the maternity department of a local store and discovered a black spandex waistband to wear over my unzippered pants and longer tops that reached the top of my thigh.

My brother, home from college, helped Jasper put the leaf in the dining room table. My husband and I took special care decorating for our Thanksgiving meal. Between the two of us, we prepared a wonderful dinner with all the fixings. Grandma made the pumpkin pies and whipped cream. Jasper's parents brought a salad.

We decided to serve the meal family-style, but before Jasper carved the turkey, he sat at the head of the table, we clasped hands, bowed our heads, and he said grace.

"Dear Lord, we thank you for this food, the roof over our head, the family gathered around this table, and the little one who will soon be joining us in June. Amen."

I grinned as I heard several numb responses as if they were trying to grasp what he said. Grandma was the first to ask.

"Elizabeth, are you expecting?"

I watched as everyone at the table looked at me with their mouths agape anticipating my reply.

I smiled and nodded my head.

"Yes, June, June 12th." I rose and joined Jasper as he stood and put his arm around my shoulders. We were surrounded by our loved ones and received hugs of congratulations. As we returned to our seats to enjoy the meal, the usual questions followed. How are you feeling? Do you know what gender you are having? What color will the nursery be painted? Do you have a nursery theme? Any names picked out?

My brother plopped a massive scoop of mashed potatoes onto his plate.

"I assume your old room will become the baby's room?" He wanted to make sure he could return to his room during semester breaks.

"That's the plan." Jasper confirmed.

Conversations around the table seemed to spark with excitement. I glanced at Jasper as I passed him the cranberries. He winked as he smiled.

Overall, the meal was a success. Grandma leaned toward me.

"Since you and Jasper did the cooking, his mom and I are going to do the dishes and put away the leftovers. Go and put your feet up."

"I'll join you in the kitchen, so you know where the clean dishes belong."

"As long as you just sit and supervise." She patted the back of my hand.

To give our full stomachs time to stop aching, some of us played cards while others visited before enjoying Grandma's pumpkin pies with whipped cream.

At the end of the evening, we escorted our guests to the door only to receive congratulations once again on our happy news.

* * *

The busy holiday season was upon us. Even though it was our first Christmas without Dad, our anticipated joy over the new addition to our family helped alleviate the sadness. Jasper and I went out to dinner on the first Saturday of December and watched the evening holiday parade in town with Santa and

Mrs. Claus on the last float. We enjoyed the tree lighting ceremony and fireworks. I imagined seeing the magic of this Christmas tradition through our child's eyes and the excitement of running to the tree on Christmas morning to see the presents left by Santa.

We decided to complete our Christmas shopping by the following week and found ourselves wandering to the infant department. The baby clothes were so tiny and cute. We decided to purchase several gifts, from Santa of course, for our baby even though we had yet to find out the gender.

Petey decided he was hungry earlier than normal on Sunday, so I relented and rose to feed the cats before church. Jasper came downstairs a few minutes later.

"Hey, I have an idea." He wrapped his arms around my ever-expanding waist.

"What?"

'Let's take a trip to Frankenmuth after church. It's only about an hour away from here. We can visit the Christmas store, have lunch, and wander through the shops. We can even get some fudge."

"Fudge. Sounds amazing."

The Christmas store was an endless display of sparkling lights, decorated trees, and too many ornaments to count. We walked through it for hours. I stopped and stared at a glass ornament of white feathers with its edges painted gold. *Mom.* I selected it from where it was displayed and placed it in the shopping basket as Jasper presented it to me as if reading my mind. I could not find an ornament to represent Dad, so I chose a colorful one of Santa since he was always so generous. After paying for our items, we enjoyed the city's famous chicken for lunch and toured the quaint shops lining the main street.

With my brother home for Christmas break, we attended midnight Mass and the three of us opened our gifts Christmas morning.

I took a plate of Christmas cookies to Grandma's for dinner and exchanged our gifts with her. I opened a gift for the baby. She made a lovely quilted blanket in neutral gender pastels of yellow, green, and white.

"Oh Grandma, it's so pretty." I traced my finger along the white lace edging and the quilting of the square blocks. "It will have a special place in the nursery. Maybe draped over the rocking chair."

"Well, it isn't only for display. I hope you use it too." She smiled.

* * *

Jasper and I were led by the nurse to the ultrasound room. She helped me lay on the table and covered my exposed abdomen with a paper sheet. Jasper held an envelope containing a blank piece of paper as we waited for the technician.

A knock sounded on the door before it opened.

"Hello." The woman entered closing the door behind her. "Let's see how your little one is doing."

She squeezed the bottle of warm goop on my abdomen, applied the instrument, and moved it around. Taking several measurements, she pressed a button to take photographs. Jasper and I watched in amazement. There was our baby. I thought I could make out its head, but maybe it was my imagination.

"See this," she pointed to the screen, "that is the heart."

"Wow." Jasper squeezed my hand.

"Everything looks good. Do you want to know the gender?"

"No, but we would like you to write it on this piece of paper for me to give to the bakery. We are going to have a baby reveal party."

The technician accepted the envelope from Jasper.

"Oh, that will be fun." She wrote the gender on the paper and handed it back to him. "I'll let you seal it." She wiped the goop from my bulbous belly. "You are all set." She handed us the paperwork to check out at the front desk before leaving the room.

It was tempting to peek inside the envelope, but Jasper licked the flap and pressed it shut before we changed our minds.

* * *

UNTIL WE MEET AGAIN

We gathered our families together for pizza, breadsticks, and salad for dinner the following weekend. It was unfortunate my brother could not come home from college to join us, so I took a video while Grandma and Jasper's mom did the honor of cutting the cake for dessert. As they lifted their pieces of cake to serve onto plates, they revealed the color of the filling. It was pink. Everyone cheered.

Jasper drew me near and kissed me.

"Looks like the nursery will be pink."

What followed was a barrage of suggestions for her name. Jasper and I had chosen her name, but we agreed not to announce it until after she was born.

* * *

My vase of feathers was placed on a bookshelf in Mom's office, now my office. I prayed the cats would leave it alone. We decorated my old bedroom in ivory, pink, and unicorns. Baby showers by families, coworkers, and friends provided the essentials. With the nursery completed, all the baby clothes washed, and plenty of disposable diapers and wipes in stock, we were ready for her arrival.

Jasper was excited about becoming a father. He often talked to my bulbous belly and laid his hand on it while we slept hoping to feel her move and kick.

I planned to work until the day I gave birth, take three months away from the office, and bring her to the office until she demanded more of my attention and I was unable to focus on my job. I visited the church's daycare and we were relieved when they agreed to hold an opening for her.

I developed the pregnant waddle and my feet swelled. I could tell when she 'dropped' because I could breathe again. My doctor's appointments became more frequent. At forty weeks, my doctor smiled as she flipped through my chart.

"I would say any day now, but babies have a mind of their own. She will get here when she is ready."

Three days later, I woke during the night with a backache and cramping. I tried to shift my body into different positions but to no relief. I got out of bed, took my phone from the charger, and went downstairs hoping not to wake Jasper. Petey and Max followed hoping they would receive their breakfast early.

I began pacing the living room floor while pushing the palms of my hands on my lower back hoping to relieve the pain. I assumed I was in labor. My water had yet to break, so I thought I had time before we needed to go to the hospital. I started timing my contractions. Seven minutes apart.

As the daylight announced the new day, Jasper came downstairs in his boxer shorts, concern masking his face as he looked at my labor face.

"What's wrong?"

"I'm in labor, or at least I think I am."

"How far apart are your contractions?"

"Five minutes apart." I placed my hand on my abdomen as another contraction began.

"Oh, crap. We have to get to the hospital." He ran upstairs to dress and grab my hospital bag from the nursery before coming back downstairs.

I was still in my pajamas and slippers when he ushered me out the door and helped me into the car. Within a few minutes, he pulled up to the hospital double doors and helped me into a wheelchair before a nurse came forward and took me to an area to check-in. Jasper arrived as the intern left the room.

"Well?"

"He is going to get my doctor. They may break my water to hurry the labor along."

After my doctor examined me, she broke my water.

"Now, we will see how long your little one will take to get here." She patted my upper arm before leaving the room.

The labor pains increased over time. There was an urgency, pressure.

"I have to push." Strange how I instinctively knew what to do.

Jasper went to retrieve the doctor, who verified my dilation.

"Go ahead and push."

***

I looked at my spirit guide and to my granddaughter's spirit guide.

"Even though Elizabeth is in pain, it will seem like a bad dream once she holds her baby in her arms." I tried to reassure myself.

My spirit guide nodded once.

"She will be born safely, right?"

He did not reply.

***

"Jasper, come by me," the doctor encouraged, "and help your daughter enter this world."

My husband released my hand and kissed my cheek before leaving my side. The doctor talked him through the delivery as he welcomed our daughter into our lives. He held her within his large hands as she inhaled her first breath.

"Wow." He looked at me, mesmerized by the miracle.

"That's my favorite part." The doctor explained. "You feel them breathing life into their tiny bodies as if their soul is entering it." The doctor placed the umbilical cord in her hand and waited for it to stop beating before clipping it in two spots. She took our baby girl from Jasper's hands. A nurse handed him a pair of scissors and he cut the cord. The doctor placed our daughter on my chest and began wiping her with a soft towel.

"Hello, Maysie Marie McLean." I traced the bridge of her nose with my finger, over her cheek, and under her chin. "She's beautiful."

Jasper kissed my forehead before lowering his face to meet hers.

"Hi, baby girl." He rested his head against my pillow as I held her, and we watched the first moments of her life together.

"Shall I get her bathed for you?" A nurse took Maysie to a padded platform heated by warming lights and surrounded by Plexiglas. Playing the role of the protective father, Jasper peered over the nurse's shoulder as she was weighed, measured, and examined before receiving a sponge bath. The nurse dressing her in a diaper and onesie.

Jasper pulled his cellphone from his pocket.

"Hey, she's here!" He looked at me. "Yes, Elizabeth is fine, a little tired, but fine. I think she is happy to have the labor over and done with." He looked at our daughter. "Yes, Maysie Marie and she is a cutie. So far, she hasn't cried much. The nurse just finished bathing her and has her dressed." He traced his knuckle over our daughter's soft cheek in awe of the miracle we created together as the nurse swaddled her in a thin blanket.

Jasper called my brother and Grandma and shared our good news with them as well. He turned to see the nurse waiting to put Maysie in his arms. He returned his phone to his back pocket and cradled her in his arms, smiled, and looked at me.

"She's so tiny."

I chuckled.

"She didn't feel tiny coming out of me, but in your arms, she looks very small."

"She's beautiful, just like her mother."

I didn't feel beautiful. My hair was sweaty, my body coated in dampness, and I wanted to take a shower. The question that formed in my mind – did I have enough strength to do so?

The nurse approached my bed.

"Your chart indicates you will be breastfeeding?"

"Yes, I want to try anyway."

The nurse coached me through the first feeding. I was amazed by my body's ability to not only give birth but to give sustenance to our daughter too. Jasper placed Maysie on his shoulder and gently patted her back to encourage her to burp while she slept.

The nurse looked at my damp hair.

"Would you like help to take a shower?"

I grinned.

"You read my mind." I rotated my legs to the side of the bed and stood as she supported me while a wave of dizziness caused me to sway. She waited until I was steady on my feet.

"Let's get you to the bathroom. There is a seat for you to sit on while you shower."

The warm water renewed my body. I dressed in a pair of pajamas I brought in my hospital bag, returned to bed, and Jasper placed Maysie in my arms.

When our celebration dinner arrived from the hospital kitchen, Jasper placed our darling daughter in the heated infant bed.

I had often overheard others talk about the lack of flavor in hospital food. I was too hungry to notice as I shoveled it into my mouth. After finishing my meal, I was still hungry and raided the snacks I packed in my bag. Why was I so hungry? Did labor increase my appetite? Did my body need additional calories for nursing? Maybe with the baby no longer pushing my organs upward, my stomach was able to finally contain a full meal.

The next morning, Jasper went home to shower and feed the cats. Maysie was napping in her bed. Since we expected Grandma, my brother, and Jasper's parents to visit later in the afternoon, I closed my eyes and fell asleep.

A nurse patted my shoulder to wake me to take my vitals. She looked at the baby in the hospital bassinette and smiled.

"You had a visitor while you were sleeping."

I glanced at the clock on the wall. It was only ten o'clock, too early for our expected company.

"Really, who?"

"He stopped at the nurses' station and said he was your father. He wanted me to tell you he couldn't stay and that you have a beautiful baby girl."

I scowled. Did I hear her correctly?

"My father?"

She smiled and nodded as she put the blood pressure cuff around my arm.

"Yes, your father."

I grabbed my phone, thumbed through the pictures until I found one of him. I held the phone before her.

"Is this him?"

"Yes, that's him alright." She finished taking my blood pressure, temperature, and checked the oxygen level in my blood before leaving the room.

I got out of bed, picked up my infant daughter, and sat in a chair. Tears blurred my vision.

"I wished you could have known your Grandma and Grandpa. I know they would have spoiled you, especially Grandpa. I imagine you would have wrapped him around your little finger." I wiped the tears cascading down my cheeks before they could drip onto the swaddled blanket.

* * *

My husband peered over our daughter's shoulder at the little one's face.

"She looks like Elizabeth, don't you think, dear."

I peeked over the edge of the blanket to see our granddaughter.

"Very similar." I went to the empty hospital bed and laid a feather on the pillow. "We must go."

* * *

Jasper walked in and kissed me. I stood and handed him Maysie before getting back into bed. I absentmindedly picked up the feather on my pillow and twirled it between my thumb and index finger.

"Guess who the nurse said stopped by this morning while I was sleeping?"

He traced his finger along Maysie's jawline before looking at me.

"You had a visitor? So early this morning? Who?"

"She said my dad stopped by while I was sleeping, said he couldn't stay, but wanted us to know that we have a beautiful baby girl."

Jasper looked at me with his eyebrows drawn close together.

"That's strange. Did the nurse know your dad had passed away?"

"No, I didn't tell her, but I showed her a picture of him on my phone. She confirmed it was him." I looked at the feather, momentarily wondering where it had come from, then remembered finding it on my pillow. I smiled assured Mom had visited me once again.

Shortly after noon, Grandma came into my hospital room with a container of homemade cookies and a gift for Maysie. She had Jasper use her cell phone to take pictures while she held her great-granddaughter. I was quite certain she would go directly to her neighbors or her friends at church and share the photographs. My brother visited after dinner. He did not want to hold her, but Jasper placed Maysie in his arms anyway. He stiffened as if frozen and afraid to move.

"I'm afraid I'm going to break her." He smiled at the wonder of her tiny face and was astonished as she freed one of her hands from her blanket, reached skyward, and clasped onto his finger. "She's to teeny."

Within a few days, the three of us arrived home and settled into a routine of sleepless nights and napping when we could.

Life as a new mom was an adventure. It's amazing what lack of sleep will do to the mind. Grandma was a great help with cooking, but her opinion on what I should and should not do needed to be taken into consideration before following through with her advice.

Jasper took to fatherhood well. He didn't mind changing diapers, walked the floor holding her against his chest when she cried, kept the house clean, and the laundry caught up.

UNTIL WE MEET AGAIN

***

Time passed quickly. Maysie grew and became more aware of her surroundings every day. It seemed too soon to wish my brother good luck as he left home and headed back to college for his second year. With Jasper back at work and coaching, it was just me, Petey, Max, and Maysie during the day. I usually had dinner on the table when Jasper arrived home after practice. His priority after kissing me as he walked in the door was to scoop Maysie into his arms to enjoyed some time with her.

With the leaves on the trees beginning to change, I started to work from home while Maysie napped. On especially lovely autumn days, I bundled her up, put her in her stroller, and we walked into town for lunch. I stopped at the office and carried her upstairs for a visit before walking home.

For Halloween, we dressed Maysie as a peanut. She was passed around and held by everyone in attendance at Thanksgiving. Our Christmas seemed more magical to see it through her eyes. After the holidays, Maysie began attending 'baby school' at our church's daycare and I returned to work full time.

Family Life

Our weekdays seemed to blur with the daily routine of getting ready for work, dropping Maysie off at daycare, working, picking Maysie up from daycare, dinner, sleep, and repeat the next day. Thank goodness for weekends when Jasper watched Maysie while doing the laundry and I ventured out to grocery shop. Other than attending church on Sunday, the rest of our weekend allowed us to regroup for the following week.

The long winter days became shorter and bowed to the emergence of spring. Jasper was busy correcting papers while our daughter slept on a Saturday afternoon, so I decided to go for a run through town.

UNTIL WE MEET AGAIN

The branches of the trees lining the historic streets of town were tipped with various budding shades of green. Yellow daffodils in flowerbeds were a welcomed sight as I jogged toward the park. People paused in raking their lawns and trimming bushes to wave as I passed. I stopped momentarily at an intersection to allow a car to pass through and saw in my peripheral vision a golden light at its base of a large oak tree next to me. It was the golden color of candlelight and the size of a salad plate. However, when I blinked and looked at it, it was not there. *Strange*? I slowed to a walk. I was quite certain I had seen the glowing light but had no reasonable explanation for what it was. Maybe it was sunlight reflecting off a lost hubcap or something? I walked around the tree, but only saw grass. I continued with my jog through the park and the return trip home. Breathing heavily as I slowed to a walk and proceeded up the driveway, my body rejuvenated from the invigorating run. Maysie crawled to me as I stepped into the kitchen.

She took her first steps a few weeks later, a milestone I was thrilled to witness. She surprised her uncle when he arrived home from college for the summer as she stood in the kitchen and greeted him at the door. She stepped toward him with her arms open wide. He looked at me.

"She's walking?" He set his garbage bag of dirty clothes on the floor and picked her up. "You are such a big girl."

Maysie giggled as he tickled her tummy.

***

Jasper tidied up his classroom and closed it down for the summer. We reduced Maysie's time at daycare to two days a week so Jasper could spend time with her and still have time for himself to do yard work, review lesson plans for the coming school year, and devise a strategy for the coming soccer season.

On the morning of Maysie's first birthday, we decorated the flower garden with balloons and streamers. Our small family gathered for a luncheon cookout. Everyone had their cameras ready as Maysie sat in her highchair and was presented with her personal-size birthday cake that resembled a large cupcake. She was timid at first, uncertain of what to do, but once she tasted the frosting, she dove in with both hands.

Throughout the summer, her vocabulary grew daily. She enjoyed playing in her small plastic swimming pool on hot days, getting sand in her hair while playing in the sandbox, and had her favorite baby doll in her hand everywhere she went.

As the summer foliage began to change with the coming season, my brother returned to college for his third year and Jasper returned to work.

My cellphone rang one evening while I was bathing Maysie before putting her down for the night. I looked at the caller ID and I wondered what my brother wanted. I lowered the toilet seat and sat while keeping a watchful eye on my daughter.

"Hey, what's up?"

"Hey. I just wanted you to know I'm coming home for the weekend. I'm bringing someone with me that I want you to meet."

"Ok, someone like who?"

"My girlfriend."

Jasper entered the bathroom as Maysie screeched. He looked at me as if curious to know who I was talking to on the phone. I tapped him on the arm as he stepped to the tub to wash Maysie.

"Oh, how long have you known this girlfriend?"

Jasper's head snapped toward me with his eyebrows raised and his mouth agape.

"We met during our freshman year, had a few classes together, and worked on a few class assignments."

I winked at Jasper.

"We look forward to meeting her."

"Ya, and she will be sleeping in my room, with me."

It was not a question he posed. It was more like a forewarning and one not open for discussion.

"So, you're asking me to change your bedsheets?" I grinned and watched Jasper lift Maysie from the bathtub and wrap her in a towel.

He hesitated.

"Good idea. Thanks. We'll see you in a few days."

"Ok, bye."

Jasper toweled the wisps of blond hair on Maysie's head.

"So, your brother has a girlfriend?"

"Yes, and he is bringing her home this weekend for us to meet her."

* * *

My brother and his girlfriend were already at the house when I arrived home from work on Friday. With Maysie on my hip as I walked in the backdoor, I placed her on the floor, and she ran to her uncle with arms opened wide. He picked her up, hugged her, and ticked her tummy causing her to giggle before introducing me to his girlfriend, who was strikingly beautiful.

I poured three glasses of lemonade before we went to the living room to visit while Maysie played with her toys. Jasper arrived home within the hour with pizza and salad for dinner.

I watched my brother and his girlfriend throughout the meal. The way they looked at each other, a random touch, and exchanged grins. She was polite, seemed to enjoy Maysie, and conversed easily. Her intellect was apparent. I often caught my brother looking at me as if trying to read my mind or an indication of my approval.

I washed Maysie's hands and face before releasing her from the highchair. Everyone helped put the dishes in the dishwasher before following our daughter to the living room. As

I put the leftover pizza in the refrigerator, my brother pulled me aside.

"Well, what do you think of her?"

I peeked into the living room at Jasper, Maysie, and his girlfriend.

"I like her, but I've only just met her. What do you think of her?"

He grinned.

"I like her too."

"How long have you two been going out?"

"Since the start of this school year."

"So, you were friends first." I nodded. "That's good. Then you must know her quite well."

"Yes, quite well."

"Are you thinking of marrying her?"

He scoffed.

"I don't think our relationship has gotten that serious. I mean, even though we met during our freshman year, we have only dated a few months. It's much too soon to talk of marriage."

Overall, the weekend with them was pleasant. My brother was the cautious type, so obtaining my opinion of his girlfriend was a needed step before fully committing his heart to the relationship.

Another Year Passes

It was hard to believe Maysie was celebrating her second birthday. So far, she has yet to reach the terrible part. Her chattering is nonstop, and she increases her vocabulary daily. As little girls often do, she screams and squeals when she is being chased or when she chases the cats. She still is attached to her baby doll and it is becoming quite ragged.

As always, our birthday dinners are low key, family only. Well, except for my brother's girlfriend, but she is practically family. We enjoyed birthday cake, ice cream, and watching Maysie open her presents. It took a while to settle her down for bed, but before long only silence could be heard in her bedroom. Grandma left for home soon afterward and we gathered around the campfire to unwind and relax. I looked at my brother sitting next to his girlfriend.

"So, your last year at college."

He looked at his girlfriend and grinned slightly.

"I'm ready to finish, graduate, and move on." He clasped her hand. "We are renting an apartment off-campus this coming year."

I wondered how Mom and Dad would have reacted to his announcement. In my opinion, I thought it would be a good way for them to discover if they were compatible.

"I hope you reserved it before you left for the summer."

"We did. We are all set."

"Any idea what the two of you will be doing after graduation? Jobwise, I mean."

"There's nothing etched in granite, but we are working on it."

* * *

I caught myself instinctively rocking from side to side with his little head cradled in the crook of my arm. He stared at me with wonder. I looked at his big sister sleeping in her baby bed.

"Pretty soon you will be sleeping in this bed and your sister will be in a big girl bed." I kissed his forehead. "Remember grandma loves you."

"And Grandpa loves you too." My husband kissed our grandson on the forehead, brought his finger with the little hand wrapped around it to his lips, and kissed the tiny fingers.

I turned and placed our grandson in his spirit guide's arms.

"I will see you again soon." I glanced at my spirit guide, who nodded once in confirmation.

* * *

"Mum, mum, mum, wakey, wakey."

I reluctantly opened my eyes and listened to Maysie chatter as she played with her doll in her crib. She sounded content for the moment. I closed my eyes and listened to her play. I assumed one day she would grow tired of waiting for me to get her from her crib and gather her courage to climb out.

The shower sounded as Jasper began his morning routine of returning to school. At least he did not have to compete for hot water with my brother who had returned to college.

"Mum, mum." The volume of her call increased. I threw back the blankets and rose from the bed quickly. I could feel the color drain from my face and my stomach became queasy as I grabbed the bedroom doorframe. A wave of lightheadedness took me by surprise.

"Good morning, baby girl." I lifted Maysie from the crib, placed her on the carpeted floor, and followed her down the stairs as she descended backward. I started the coffee and sat in a kitchen chair. I patted my face and my cheeks were clammy. I took a few deep breaths. The last time I felt like this I was... oh, my. Could I be pregnant?

I managed to get Maysie in her highchair. I gave her some dry cereal to munch on while I made toast.

Jasper came downstairs dressed for work.

"Good morning." He kissed my forehead and turned to Maysie. "Good morning little lady." He kissed her too. Noticing I had not replied to his cheerful greeting, he looked at my ashen face.

"You OK? You don't look so good."

My eyelids drooped. I tried to smile but only exhaled.

"Either I have the flu, or I'm pregnant." I chuckled teasingly.

Jasper smiled.

"I hope it's the latter of the two." He grinned as he grabbed the toast as it popped up from the toaster and buttered it while I took my cup of coffee and sat at the table next to Maysie's highchair.

With his sack lunch under his arm and a full travel mug of coffee in hand, he set the plate of toast on the table, kissed us both good-bye, and left for work.

I moved lethargically, sitting often, and breathing deeply as I dressed Maysie and myself for the day. After dropping her off at daycare, I lumbered up the stairs to my office with only a pack of saltine crackers in my purse for lunch.

The secretary took one look at me as I stepped into the room.

"Oh, you aren't feeling very well this morning, are you?"

"I've felt better. I may have the flu. If I get any worse, I'll go home." Even though my stomach did not improve, I managed to soldier through the workday.

Jasper made chili for dinner. The aroma turned my stomach. I couldn't eat it. I couldn't even go into the kitchen. He brought me two slices of buttered toast while I laid down on the couch and watched TV while he and Maysie ate. He stepped into the living room.

"Do you need anything else?" He set a glass of ice water on the end table.

"No, thank you."

"Still feeling bad?"

"Not my best."

"A few of my students have been out with the flu, so it's going around at school."

"I guess time will tell." I had yet to miss my period.

He placed the palm of his hand on my forehead.

"You don't have a fever."

"Maybe I'll feel better in the morning."

Unfortunately, I didn't. My stomach was still a little queasy, and even though I slept well, I was tired.

As I walked past the secretary on my way to my office, she looked at me with an all-knowing smirk on her face.

"Still not feeling well?"

I sighed.

"No, about the same."

"If I didn't know any better, I think your face says it all."

I stopped and turned toward her as I stood in my office doorway.

"My face?"

"Yes, the mask of pregnancy?" She tilted her head and grinned.

My eyebrows drew together as I mentally counted the weeks.

"Jasper said the flu is going around at school. If I don't have the flu, then I guess it may be a possibility." I went to my desk calendar and looked for the 'x' I put on the first day of my period. I was right in my calculations, but doubt settled within my mind.

Over the next few weeks, my monthly time failed to show. I went to the doctor and my pregnancy was confirmed. I left work early, picked up Maysie from daycare, and went home to make dinner. I had a craving for pancakes, eggs, and bacon. Jasper stepped in the door as I placed the last dish on the table.

"Oh, I smell bacon."

"I had a craving for a big breakfast."

"Da, Da." Maysie shoved a sticky bite of pancake into her mouth as Jasper kissed the top of her head before kissing me.

"How are you feeling?"

"Pregnant."

Jasper froze with his hand on the back of his chair. He turned toward me.

"Pregnant?"

I nodded and smiled.

He smiled as he pulled me into his arms.

"Looks like your brother will be sharing his room with the baby."

"I'm not due until after he graduates from college. We have time to work out the details long before the baby arrives. Besides, the baby will sleep in the bassinet in our bedroom for the first few months."

* * *

My hips hurt as I waddled down the aisle of the auditorium in search of three consecutive open seats. With only a month to go in my pregnancy, I was forewarned our little boy was not so little. It was a message he conveyed frequently as he kicked my ribs, which took my breath away. He rested against my spine causing my back to ache as well. Overall, he was running out of room.

I packed lots of snacks for Maysie to eat and two new small toys to play with during the graduation ceremony, a bribe to keep her quiet and content.

"How about these seats, Elizabeth?" Grandma stopped behind me at the end of a row. I nodded and followed her as she entered. She sat to my left and Jasper to my right with our daughter in his lap.

The ceremony lengthened into over an hour. Maysie was passed between the three of us with the hope of keeping her content until the end.

When my brother's name was announced, we cheered and clapped as he crossed the stage and accepted his diploma. We did the same for his girlfriend as she accepted her diploma too.

My hips were stiff when I rose from my seat. I groaned. Jasper turned toward me and picked up Maysie as she held her arms upward.

"Are you OK?"

"Yes, just a little stiff. I feel like the Tinman in the Wizard of Oz. I need an oil can to lubricate my hips so I can move again."

We followed the crowd out of the auditorium, into the sunshine, and waited on the lush green lawn for my brother to join us. Dressed in his cap and gown, he led his girlfriend toward us. We greeted them both with hugs and handshakes of congratulations and were introduced to her family who stood behind her. Photographs were taken followed by dinner at a restaurant. My brother announced he and his girlfriend were moving from their apartment off-campus to an apartment close to home to give us more room for the baby. They had interviewed with various companies, secured employment, and would begin their jobs the following week. They planned to continue their education online to earn their master's degrees.

The next morning, I tossed aside the blankets, stood from the bed, and realized I could breathe. The baby had dropped lower in my abdomen. My feet were more swollen than when I carried Maysie. As far as I was concerned, this little guy could enter this world today, but he had his own agenda.

Once my brother's room was empty, we painted and decorated, moved the crib into the new nursery, and set up my brother's bed in Maysie's room. She was excited to have a big girl bed. We put a baby gate at the top of the stairs in case she should get out of bed during the night. The newborn clothing and blankets I saved in plastic bins were washed and ready for our son's arrival. Several of Grandma's friends at church made blankets in little boy colors. A particularly pretty one was draped over the back of the rocking chair in his room.

Our son arrived two days after his due date. As the doctor predicted, he weighed in three ounces over ten pounds.

Expanding Our Family

With both babies in bed for the night and my monitor in hand, I relaxed in the lounge chair and looked at the indigo sky dotted with stars as the four of us sat around the campfire.

"Marshmallow?" My brother pointed at me while holding the roasting stick with two golden-brown marshmallows on the tips of the prongs.

I shook my head.

"No, thanks. I've had enough." I looked at the monitor as I heard the hunger cry of the baby. "I'll be right back."

After nursing, burping, and laying the little man back in his bassinet, I came downstairs and entered the kitchen to find my brother waiting for me.

"Need something?" I paused before going back to the campfire.

"Just your opinion."

He seemed jittery as he paced the floor and ran his hand through his hair pulling it back away from his eyes.

"Sounds serious."

"You like her, right?"

"Your girlfriend. Yes, I like her."

"I'm going to ask her to marry me." His smile was hesitant as if waiting for my reply.

I smiled.

"It's your choice. Good."

His tentative smile faded.

"What do you mean by that?"

"I mean it is your choice, your decision. Yes, I like her, but I don't have to live with her."

He scowled.

"What's that supposed to mean?"

He was seeking my approval. I tried to sound reassuring as I helped him search his heart.

"Do you love her?"

"Yes."

I detected a defensive tone in his reply.

"Is your life better with her in it?"

He sighed, calming himself.

"Yes."

"Do you see yourself spending the remainder of your life with her, sharing each other's successes and failures, good times and bad until death do you part?"

He smiled, almost chuckled as I mimicked the sermon of a priest.

"Yes."

"Then there is your answer. You have made your choice."

He persisted.

"But do you like her?"

I sighed as I smiled.

"Yes, very much. She is ambitious, organized, and assertive. She enjoys the children too. I can see she compliments you fully, fulfills your life, and you enjoy each other's company."

"OK." He nodded and turned to leave.

"Have you asked her father for her hand in marriage?"

He froze with his foot in midair, turned, and scowled as he looked at me.

"Oh, god, do you mean I have to?"

"Yes, out of respect."

"Isn't that a little old fashioned?"

"No."

He sighed.

"Fine."

"Do you know how you are going to propose?"

"I have a few ideas."

"Don't forget to get down on one knee. Mom told me Dad didn't get down on his knee when he proposed, and she always felt jilted out of a proper proposal."

"I'll be sure to do so."

"Do you have a ring?"

"Yes. She pointed out several while we were shopping one day. I think she will be happy with what I purchased, but the jeweler said if she doesn't like it, we can trade it in for a different one."

"Nice."

"Well, thanks for the advice. I'll let you know once I pop the question."

* * *

I changed the month on my calendar to October, my favorite month. Who doesn't love the colorful foliage of the trees, apple cider and fresh warm donuts from the cider mill, cornstalks, Indian corn, and pumpkins? With a crispness in the air, the leaves rustled under my feet as I went for a run in town. Today was Mom's birthday. Another reason for me to get some exercise and be alone with my thoughts. It had been a while since I had thought of her, but this day will always be remembered as her day, and the day Jasper rescued Max. As I entered the park, I thought of the traditions we had as children;

visiting the candy store, fishing in the park, and setting out our lawn chairs to watch free concerts performed from the gazebo. The highlight of our summer was watching the 4th of July parade dressed in our red, white, and blue clothes and crazy hats. In the winter, an evening parade with its floats and marching bands decorated in twinkling lights, Santa and Mrs. Claus riding on the last float, and the illumination of the Christmas Tree at the community center. It saddened my heart that Mom and Dad missed witnessing the events through the children's eyes, their wonder and excitement as they pointed to something they have not seen before.

Making my way back to the house, my phone rang. The caller ID indicated it was my brother.

"Hey." I stopped at the corner of an intersection to wait for traffic to clear. I glanced at the base of the tree where I had previously seen the glowing orb. Nothing was there.

"I thought you should be the first to know."

I could hear the excitement in his voice as I tried to catch my breath.

"OK."

"I asked her to marry me."

"What did she say?" The sarcasm thick in the tone of my reply.

He laughed.

"She said yes. We discussed it and we would like to have a small ceremony in Mom's flower garden just like you and Jasper did. Is that OK?"

The garden was bedded down for the winter.

"I assume you would like to have your wedding during warmer months?"

"Yes, sometime this spring or summer. We have yet to set a date."

I would have to do some weeding and planting to have the garden looking its best.

"Sure, I think that would be nice. Will the reception be at the house as well?"

"Yes, we want to keep it simple and save our money for a house."

"I think that's a good idea. Well, congratulations. I am happy for you both."

"Thanks.

"Don't forget to call Grandma and tell her the good news."

"I will. Bye."

"Bye." I stared at my phone as I hung up the call and stepped into the intersection.

Tires squealed. Someone yelled. It was as if my surroundings and I were moving in slow motion. I glanced at the oncoming car and the look of panic on the driver's face before

UNTIL WE MEET AGAIN

my body was slammed to the pavement. My eyes closed and I surrendered to the blackness of the unknown.

Not My Time

Surrounded by darkness, I saw a pinpoint of light in the distance. As I went toward it, it enlarged, and I squinted my eyes as it became lightning brighter. I stepped from the darkness into the light and placed my feet upon the floor of a room, or at least I thought it was a room. I could not see any walls, just endless whiteness. Did it go on forever? I blinked my eyes allowing them to adjust to the brightness. I grinned as I sighed.

"I'm home." I looked about the room. There was a man in a white robe standing opposite me a short distance away. His back was toward me, his head bowed as if he was reading something. Shoulder length chestnut hair with flecks of blonde highlights hung in waves on his head. He raised his head ever so slowly yet did not turn around to face me. It was Him.

I was disappointed. No, it was anger. How could I be angry with Him, yet I was.

"Why won't you show me your face? I want to see your face."

The man sighed. Still, he did not turn around.

"I cannot show you my face. If I did, you would not want to return. It is not your time."

His voice was calm and comforting as if I have always known him. I scowled, confused as my anger subsided.

"My time?"

"It is not your time to join us. You must return."

"But what if I want to stay here?"

"You cannot."

Was I dreaming? This place seemed familiar, yet unfamiliar at the same time.

"If it is not my time, then why am I here?"

"You have been chosen to relay two messages."

"Chosen?"

He continued without explanation.

"The first message is for those who are unable to attend church. I care little for the stipanations and rules of such religions. What matters most to me is everyone loves me in their heart."

I nodded my head tilting it to one side. How could I argue with his reasoning? Would I continue to attend church? Yes.

"And the second?"

"Is for a woman you know. Her heart is heavy with grief. Her son was murdered several years ago."

I scanned my mind trying to determine who He was talking about. I sighed.

"That's horrible. How old was he?"

"He was in his early twenties. Please tell her that her son is fine and happy. He watches over his mother and is proud of the difficult choices she has made and how she continues to move forward with her life without him."

I had to pose the question.

"Do I know this person?"

"Yes. You see her quite often."

Had I been so blind not to recognize when someone was grieving? How she may be suffering, had been through? Was I so self-centered and selfish that I had not considered what others may be experiencing in their life? I stared at the back of the man's head, dumbfounded.

"Who?"

"The secretary where you are employed."

How many times had I passed by her desk, her chipper face greeting me on my best and worst days, and all the while she masked her grief? Mom had not mentioned her tragedy, nor had Dad. Had they known about her son's death, or had she kept it a secret from them as well?

The man began to walk away, but his voice resonated over his shoulder.

"When you awake, you will be uninjured. It is time for you to go, but we will meet again someday."

My heart seemed to fill with joy, gratitude, and love. I sighed and my smile reflected the emotions within me. I looked at a pair of strong hands gripping my left shoulder and upper arm. My smile faded as I recognized them. *Dad*? A second pair gripped my right shoulder and upper arm. I stared in disbelief. *Mom*? I was pushed back into the darkness. The light quickly reduced to a pinpoint once again.

"She's back." A voice announced as I opened my eyes. People were gathered around me as I lay on the asphalt road. They picked up my body, placed me on a stretcher, and loaded me into an ambulance.

"I'm fine." No one would listen to me. "I'm fine. I need to go home."

A paramedic got into the back of the ambulance and began taking my pulse.

"We're just going to take you to the hospital and get you checked out. You gave us quite a scare."

"Where's my phone?"

The paramedic reached into his pocket, withdrew it, and handed it to me.

"The police have already contacted your husband. He will meet us at the hospital."

Jasper was pacing in front of the emergency doors as the ambulance pulled up and peered over the shoulders of the paramedics as they rolled the stretcher out of the back.

"My god, Elizabeth, what happened?"

A paramedic began chattering as a doctor stepped through the double doors.

"She coded but seems unharmed. BP and vitals are normal."

Jasper's head snapped toward me as he walked beside the stretcher.

"You died?"

"Yes, but I don't know for how long. I'm fine. They just have to give me the once over and then we can go home." A thought occurred to me. "Where are the kids?"

"I took them to your grandma's. I have to call her with an update once the doctor is done."

As He had stated, I was unharmed and was wheeled out of the emergency room three hours later with two important messages to share.

Sharing His Message

The first message was easy to share. All I had to do is tell Grandma, who told nearly everyone at church. As they say, the fastest form of communication is word of mouth. Others approached me after Mass to hear my story firsthand. I wondered if the administrators of the church were offended by His message. No matter, I continued to spread it to those who would listen. I created a website of some of my experiences in dealing with the loss of my parents, visions, and dreams. Oh, yes, and the feathers I discover. Maybe I was on a mission to help people believe in the afterlife and of His love for every one of us.

I went into work on Monday uncertain how my secretary would react to what I had to say. I climbed the oak stairs and rehearsed the details of what I needed to convey in my mind.

"Good morning, Elizabeth." She was her normal cheerful self.

"Good morning." I walked the few paces to my office and placed my hand on the doorknob.

"My, I heard you had quite a weekend. Such a terrible thing. Didn't the driver see you?"

I turned to look at her.

"I think it was more like I didn't see him."

"Are you all right? No broken bones?"

"I'm completely healthy." I turned the knob, pushed the door open, and paused. His message would have to be delivered sooner or later. I might as do it now. "Do you have a minute to come into my office?"

"Oh, sure." She sprang from her chair and marched past me through the open door.

I took a deep breath as I closed the door behind me. I knew what I had to say was for her ears only. I placed my lunch bag in my college refrigerator that I kept behind my desk next to the credenza and glanced at my displayed photographs before turning and placing my purse in the bottom right drawer of my desk.

"It seems everyone in town has heard about my accident. Quite foolish, really. But many have not heard what I am about to tell you." I motioned for her to sit in one of the two chairs before my desk. I sat next to her in the other. "What have you heard so far?"

"That you died, went through a dark tunnel, and saw God in a room that was filled with bright light."

"Yes."

"And that he gave you the message that we are to love Him with all of our hearts."

"Yes, but what many do not know is that I have a specific message for you."

Her eyebrows raised.

"For me?"

"Yes. I was told you carry a burden with you, one of grief. Your son was murdered several years ago."

Her eyes pooled with tears. She nodded her head slightly, wanting to look away from my face, yet wanting to hear what I had to say. I smiled slightly hoping to ease the impact of what I was about to tell her.

"He indicated the message is from your son. He wants you to know that he is fine and happy, he is proud of the difficult choices you have had to make, and how you have continued with your life without him."

Her bottom lip quivered as tears cascaded down her cheeks. I was not sure if her tears were of joy or sorrow. However, I like to believe our tears for our departed loves ones represent the love we have for them. I reached for the box of tissues on my desk and presented it to her. She removed several and blotted her face.

"Did you see my son?"

"No, but I hope you receive comfort from what the message conveyed."

She looked down in her lap at the crumpled, damp facial tissues in her hands.

"He was so young. He had his whole life ahead of him." She looked at me. "He was studying to be a pediatric oncologist. He loved children and wanted to cure their cancer." She sighed. "He was in the wrong place at the wrong time." She began to cry in earnest.

I touched her shoulder and waited for her to compose herself.

"I'm sorry to have upset you."

She blew her nose and looked at me.

"Don't apologize. He knew what I needed to hear. Thank you."

I nodded and looked at the paperwork awaiting me on my desk, but knew my secretary needed time to pull herself together.

"I have to go to the warehouse for a moment. Take as much time as you need in the privacy of my office to think over what I said. If you need to, take the day off. We can answer the phones."

She stood as I did and embraced me.

"Thank you."

"You're welcome." I left the room closing the door behind me.

The Wedding

My brother and his fiancé chose the second Saturday in June as their wedding date, which gave me enough time to ensure the flower garden looked its best. I wondered if her family was displeased by their daughter not following the tradition of getting married in her hometown, which was out of state. Since she and her family were unfamiliar with our city establishments and services, I advised and assisted in the preparations when asked and respectfully stepped aside to allow this milestone to be shared between my future sister-in-law and her mother. I arranged for the tent and the caterer, verifying it served the items the happy couple wished to have on the menu. Her parents flew into town a few days before the wedding and stayed at a hotel. Being of Scottish descent, the wedding colors were those of their family tartan. Their centerpieces for the tables contained a single thistle nestled among the arrangements. I was informed her wedding dress would display their family tartan on her skirt and bodice. Even though her father would wear a kilt for the ceremony, my brother refused to comply.

It rained for three days straight the week of the wedding. Wanting the event to be perfect for his bride, my brother, the nervous groom, called me often expressing his concern about the ceremony.

"The weather is supposed to be nice for Saturday, but do you think we should rent a second tent for the flower garden?"

I kept my voice calm.

"I have talked to the tent company. They are on standby to set up another tent if the need should arise."

Rays of sunshine peeked over the horizon the morning of their wedding. Unfortunately, the temperature and humidity rose to an uncomfortable level as well.

I stood with my arms folded over my chest and scanned the flower garden before looking at the tent for the reception. I was thankful the tent company had the foresight to bring several fans to circulate the humid air.

"Well, are we ready?"

I turned around to see my brother exiting the house.

"Yes, are you?"

"Absolutely." He looked at the yard in all its splendor. "It looks great. Thanks for your help."

"You are welcome, but most of it was done by your bride and future mother-in-law."

In the late afternoon, we seated ourselves in the flower garden and waited for the bride and her father to appear. My brother stood near the priest and another official by the arbor. He nervously pulled the sleeves of his jacket toward his wrist to straighten them. Our eyes met as he glanced at me, straightened his tie, and grinned. I returned his smile hoping to ease his nervousness.

The bagpiper began to play a lovely tune as the ceremony began. Everyone stood as the bride and her father appeared at the end of the short aisle. Her dress was made of ivory satin with a full skirt and a strapless corset bodice. It was embellished with a tartan overskirt and the same material draped over one shoulder. Dressed in a tux jacket, white shirt, and vest, her father's kilt was the same tartan material. They preceded up the aisle, her father kissed her on the cheek and gave her hand to my brother before taking his seat next to his wife as the bagpiper completed his song.

"Dearly beloved," the priest began. I listened to the identical ceremony Jasper and I had years ago. I looked at Jasper as he held Maysie, and I tried to entertain our son on my lap.

"Sound familiar?" I whispered.

He looked at me with a silly grin on his face.

"Best day of my life. It ranks right up there with each day our children were born."

* * *

Pride. Joy. My heart was fulfilled as I watched my children and listened to the ceremony.

"He looks so happy." I looked at my husband standing next to me. Our spirit guides stood nearby waiting patiently as always.

"They were destined to be so, and I wish them all the best." He turned his head toward me, smiled, and clasped my hand. "We did good, you and me. Perhaps we can do it once again sometime in the future."

I nodded as I blew a white feather in the air and listened as the ceremony continued.

* * *

A feather floated down from above my head and landed in my lap. I smiled as I picked it up and tickled my son's nose with it before redirecting my attention to the other presiding official as she began to speak. A bluebird landed on the top of the arbor and rotated its head as if looking at the guests before flying away. I grinned as I thought of Dad. I watched as the couple joined their forearms and a braided ribbon made of the family's tartan colors was tied around their arms. As a forewarning, my brother explained their ceremony would include handfasting which is usually performed for an engaged couple as a sign of commitment to each other. Any children born during the engagement period are considered legitimate. But since they were not handfasted during their engagement, they decided to have it as part of their ceremony in respect of her heritage.

The ceremony finished as most weddings do, with a kiss and the announcement of the married couple as man and wife. The bagpiper played a peppy tune as the bride and groom walked down the aisle. After everyone congratulated the happy couple, the guests went to the tent for refreshments while photographs were taken. The reception involved music and plenty of alcohol. I was thankful her parents provided the adult beverages and bartender.

With the party continuing well into the night, Jasper and I put the children to bed ensuring they were asleep before we rejoined the celebration. I chuckled as I watched my brother dance a fast song. I did not know he had it in him or maybe it was the alcohol he consumed that enhanced his fancy footwork.

As the celebration came to an end, gifts were loaded into the newlyweds' car and they returned to their apartment for the night. They planned to leave the next morning for a long weekend in the northern part of the state for their honeymoon.

Jasper and I fell into bed after surviving the long day. The children, with their never-adjusting internal clocks, would wake us at an early hour. My husband was asleep before his head hit the pillow. I wish I knew his secret of falling asleep so quickly as I lay awake listening to his rhythmic breathing.

Good Times

The newlyweds returned home and adjusted to married life, not that it was much different from what they knew before. We agreed to have dinner together once a week to visit as a family. The convenience of having my brother and his wife nearby also allowed Jasper and me an occasional date night without the children.

On the Fourth of July, the six of us dressed in our red, white, and blue, and crazy hats. The children sat in their red wagon and we walked to town to avoid the aftermath of traffic. We placed our chairs along the street to save a spot for viewing the parade and went to the community center to have our traditional pancake breakfast sponsored by the Lions Club.

UNTIL WE MEET AGAIN

After watching the many floats, marching bands, and way too many political leaders solicit everyone's support, we went to the park and ate a chicken dinner for lunch before walking home. After the children woke from their naps, they played in their plastic swimming pool before enjoying hamburgers and hot dogs cooked on the grill for dinner with homemade potato salad and watermelon.

I packed a picnic basket with snacks and our favorite beverages while Jasper bathed and dressed the children for bed. The six of us climbed into our SUV and drove to the park to view the fireworks. It wasn't long before the children's eyelids grew heavy with sleep. I cringed at each explosion, especially when feeling the impact of the firework in my chest, and was astonished the noise did not wake the children as they slept on a blanket on the lawn.

Arriving home, we tucked the children in bed and finished our family day around the campfire. Aware of the small nest egg my brother received from my parents, I thought to inquire.

"So, when do you think you will be able to purchase a house?"

"We are tied to our apartment lease for a year. Maybe after Christmas, we can begin looking for a house, find one to our liking, and move in by spring."

As luck would have it, they found the perfect house in January and took possession a month later, which allowed them time to paint, carpet, and move in slowly before making the final transition.

With the spring flowers in full bloom, I took the children outside to play while I worked in the flower garden. Maysie squealed drawing my attention. I pulled a weed and paused to see what caused her alarm. I was not quite certain what they were pretending to be but admired their imaginative antics of what resembled them imitating cats. I assumed Maysie was mimicking Petey.

We decided to walk into town and purchase ice cream after dinner on the unusually warm Sunday. The children went to bed and after a long day of working in the yard, I was eager to get some sleep too. I think it was the only time I fell asleep as soon as my head rested on my pillow.

~

A baby's face, cute and chubby, flashed within my mind. He was staring at me.

"He has her eyes." The thought resonated within my mind.

~

I opened my eyes as I heard one of the children stir, knowing they would wake soon. Glancing at the window, dawn was breaking. I allowed my eyelids to close hoping for a few more minutes of sleep but my mind refused to allow me the pleasure as the baby's face I saw in my dream reappeared in my memory. Her eyes? My sister-in-law's eyes? Was she expecting a baby?

Jasper's alarm rang. As he readied for work, I went to the kitchen with the children and cats in tow to start the day.

After dropping off the children at daycare, I called my sister-in-law.

"So, are you expecting a baby?"

She giggled.

"No, we're not pregnant. Why do you ask?"

I considered telling her about my dream but doubted she would believe me.

"Just wondering."

Three months later, we gathered for our weekly family dinner. My brother clasped his wife's hand in his and looked at us.

"We have an announcement." He waited until we were all looking at him. "We are expecting a baby."

"I knew it." I smiled as I looked at my sister-in-law. "It's a boy and his eyes are like yours."

Everyone looked at me as if I were crazy.

I just smiled and nodded my head confidently.

"I guess time will tell if I'm right."

Her pregnancy went smoothly. She did not suffer from morning sickness and her labor was minimal, which made me a little envious. As I held my nephew in my arms, I compared my brother's baby picture to his wife's baby picture, tilted my head, and gave them my all-knowing grin. My brother nodded.

"You're going to make me say it, aren't you?"

"Yes."

My brother sighed.

"You're right. He has her eyes."

I nodded.

"And he is beautiful."

Jasper and I tucked our children into bed that evening. Even though the challenges of parenthood awaited my brother and his wife, we were thankful to have successfully potty trained our son and looked forward to other milestones both of our children would achieve.

Busy As Usual

Days turned into weeks and weeks turned into years. Maysie started second grade and our little guy began kindergarten as the summer turned into autumn. It seemed like only yesterday when they were born. Daycare was no longer needed. On most days, I left work when they were released from school and picked them up. On occasion, we would stop at the candy store for a surprise bag and spend some time in the park. If I needed to stay later at the office, I would call the school and simply have them attend latchkey until I was able to pick them up.

After dinner one evening, I began the bathwater for the children's bath. Our son ran into the bathroom, ripped off his clothes, and jumped into the tub with only several inches of water in the bottom.

"Maysie! Bath time!" I waited for her to reply but received none. "Maysie!" Silence. Jasper came bounding up the stairs.

"She is looking at the pictures in the photo books again. I'll bathe him while you try to pull her away."

I went downstairs to discover she had indeed pulled the photo album out from beneath the coffee table and sat cross-legged on the carpet with the album in her lap.

"Honey, it's time for your bath."

"I know, but can I take my bath without my brother. I am getting older, you know."

I smiled.

"Sure." I peeked over her shoulder. "What are you looking at?"

"Pictures of Grandma and Grandpa."

I sat down next to her and looked at the photograph of my mother in her usual 'hello' pose. Her shoulders drawn up toward her head and wiggling her fingers at the camera as she waved. I sighed. It had been a while since I looked at the pictures. Maysie pointed her dainty finger at Mom in one of the photographs.

"She loves me."

For a second, I wondered how she had come to that conclusion since she had never met Mom. I smiled.

"Yes, she loves you." I heard our rambunctious little boy bouncing around upstairs. "Your brother is out of the tub. It's your turn for a bath." I tapped the edge of the album with my finger. "We can look at the pictures another time."

Maysie reluctantly return the photo album to its proper place and followed me upstairs.

* * *

I went from room to room. Their house was perfect for their growing family. Even though it needed a few improvements, my son and his wife were updating and making it their own.

I hovered next to the baby's bed and looked at his face. *Such a sweet little boy*. He had just celebrated his second birthday. He looked like my son when he was little, except for his eyes. He possessed such a delightful and entertaining personality, endless energy, and was quite intelligent for his age. I passed through the railing of the crib and kissed his cheek.

"Grandma loves you very much. I will see you very soon, but not as I am."

I went to my son's bedroom and gazed upon him and his wife. I had made my choice and was eager to begin again.

Closing my eyes, I thought of my daughter's house and envisioned her youngest child's bedroom. Opening my eyes upon my arrival, I looked down at my sleeping grandson, his face so innocent and precious. I traced my finger along his soft cheek before kissing it.

"Farewell, little one. Until we meet again."

His eyes fluttered open. He grinned and reached toward me.

"Go back to sleep, sweetheart. I must go, but please remember I love you." I kissed his outstretched palm, cupped his face within my hand as his eyes closed, and he returned to sleep. I looked at his spirit guide standing on the other side of the bed knowing he would watch over him always. I nodded respectfully trusting in his ability to do so.

I went to my granddaughter's room and looked at her sprawled body upon her bed. She was growing so quickly and possessed a lot of Elizabeth's characteristics, both physically and personality-wise. Brushing aside a strand of her hair, I kissed her forehead.

"I love you, Maysie. I have the greatest expectation for an adventurous and wonderful life for you."

I went to my former bedroom and could hear my son-in-law snoring as I entered. As I looked down at him, I was thankful his path in life led him to Elizabeth. His love for her was strong, unwavering, and eternal. His loyalty and protective nature would remain steadfast throughout their lives. He was a natural at fatherhood, always teaching and nurturing the children.

UNTIL WE MEET AGAIN

Going to the other side of the bed, I smiled as Elizabeth's face came into view. She had become such a strong and responsible young woman, a loving wife to her husband, and a patient mother. I thought of our relationship. Strange, how there seems to be an invisible bond between a mother and a daughter like a golden thread that attaches them throughout their time together and beyond.

"*Are you ready to begin again?*" My spirit guide stood loyally beside me. "*There is still more you must learn.*"

I glanced at him.

"I want to say a final farewell first."

He nodded once before I closed my eyes.

~

I lay on a bench with my head in her lap. We had spent so many days together here in the park fishing and eating the candy from our surprise bags. I listen to the water flowing over the dam as the sun warms my face. I look up into the loving eyes of my mother, who was stroking my hair. She smiles at me.

"I won't be able to visit you anymore."

Mom's face was not sad. She was smiling.

I enjoyed her visits, the feeling of her being close to me.

"Why? I like it when you visit me, and I know you are nearby when I find a white feather like the one, I assume, you left on your desk after your funeral."

"You will no longer find feathers from me. You see, I have much still to learn."

I frowned.

"Learn? I don't understand."

"Don't be sad. There is a part of me that will always be with you. You have memories and my love I have instilled within your heart."

"If you are no longer able to visit me, where will you be?"

Mom grinned from ear to ear.

"I'm so excited. I'm getting reborn."

"Reborn?"

"I am beginning my next life."

"When?"

"Well, the nonphysical time is different from your physical time, so it is difficult for me to associate the two. For me, it will be soon, but to you, it may be a while before I am in a physical state once again. A year? Maybe longer?"

"So, you are becoming physical again, like me?"

Yes, I have readied myself to begin again and have chosen my parents. I will be near you, but not know you, nor will you perceive it is me in my new life."

"So, I will know you, but not know it is you."

"Yes, you see we live many lives. With each life, we take our emotions and memories to the next life. Each life has a purpose, whether it is to teach someone something, learn something, or both. Death is just the beginning."

"The beginning." I parroted trying to comprehend the concept.

"Yes, our souls never die. Once our purpose is fulfilled in one life, we simply move onto the next with a preordained purpose."

I sat up and looked at the ducks swimming in the pond. Mom clasped my hand.

"Be happy for me and always know that I will be near. I just won't know you."

I looked down at our clasped hands. Mom and I had always been close. Her spiritual visits were comforting. Knowing I would never have another visit from her for the rest of my life made me feel hollow inside. I looked at her loving face, casting it to my memory.

"I will miss you."

"And I you." Mom placed the palm of her hand on the side of my face. "I love you."

"I love you too, Mom."

She kissed the center of my forehead bidding me farewell.

"Rest assured, your father will be watching over you until he is reborn as well."

~

I opened my eyes as a tear cascaded from the corner and disappeared into the hairline above my ear and looked at my clock on the nightstand. It was just before six o'clock. Jasper and the children were still asleep. I pushed back the covers, swung my feet over the side of the bed, and smiled at the white feather lying between my slippers. Knowing it was the last one I would find from Mom, I picked it up and rolled it between my index finger and thumb twirling it about. *Thanks, Mom.* I shoved my feet into each slipper, put on my robe, and peeked my head into the children's room to verify they were still asleep before going downstairs with both cats anticipating an early breakfast. I went to my office and dropped the feather into the vase on the bookshelf. I stood staring at the feathers representing Mom's visitations, a time she was near me, guiding, encouraging, and advising.

"Hey, what are you staring at?"

Jasper stood in the doorway of my office in his underwear leaning against the frame.

I looked at him. My grin was tinged with sadness.

"I had a dream about Mom, but I think it was more like a vision. As I got out of bed, I found a feather on the floor by my slippers. I assume it is the last one I will find from her."

"Last?" He stepped into the room, stood behind me, and placed both of his hands upon my shoulders.

"Yes, she said she is going to be reborn and won't be able to visit me anymore, but Dad will be watching over me."

Jasper leaned close to my ear.

"I'll be watching over you too." He nuzzled my cheek before placing a gentle kiss upon it.

My melancholy mood was lifted. I turned in his arms and wrapped mine around his neck.

"I can always rely on you to do so. And I will be watching over you as well." I tapped my finger on the end of his nose before pulling his face toward mine and placing a kiss on his lips.

We looked toward the stairway as the pitter-patter of little feet upon its treads echoed. We unlocked our embrace and went to the kitchen to join the children for breakfast and feed the cats.

Beginning Again

I retrieved my journal from my desk drawer, turned to the first blank page, and entered the dream of my Mom's farewell visitation. The children were asleep for the night, so I was able to take the time to recall every detail, every word of our conversation. I set my pen down and reread the entry knowing it would always be here to revisit when needed. Thumbing through the pages, I scanned each date and content. Many of my visions included Mom, while others did not. I assumed she was instrumental in initiating my dreams when she was in it. I could not help but wonder who had instilled the other visions? A higher power? One who knows all?

"Are you coming to bed?"

UNTIL WE MEET AGAIN

I looked at Jasper as he entered my office.

"Yes, I'll be right up." I returned my journal to the desk drawer, turned off the lamp, and followed him upstairs. Even though I was tired, I tossed and turned until my eyelids grew heavy and I drifted off to sleep.

~

I was in a room facing a baby's crib. I peeked over the wooden spindle railing to see a newborn infant. It was dressed in a midnight blue velvet sleeper embellished with delicate white snowflakes. It was sleeping, as babies often do, with its cheek lying on the mattress and its little chubby face turned toward me, its arms tucked under its chest, and knees drawn up under its stomach causing its little rump to lift skyward. I watched as a giant hand reached over the baby's back, the palm extended beneath the baby's stomach, and scooped him up like a bucket of a backhoe while the precious baby continued to sleep.

~

I opened my eyes to the darkness of my bedroom. Looking at my nightstand, the clock read three in the morning. I lay awake listening to Jasper's rhythmic breathing as I recalled the vision within my mind.

A baby? I knew I was not expecting. Jasper and I had planned to have only two children. However, a third would always be welcome. I wondered who could be expecting a baby soon. Blue velvet sleeper? Perhaps the baby is a boy? Snowflakes. Maybe a baby born during the winter? Strange. I promised myself to remember the dream in the morning as I synced my breathing with my husband's and drifted back to sleep.

It seemed as if I had just closed my eyes before I was pulled from my sleep and heard my son's voice.

"Mom, can we have pancakes for breakfast?" I cracked my eyes open to see his nose within an inch of mine as he rested his chin on the mattress. I could not think of a better way to begin a Saturday morning.

"Sure. Pancakes sound amazing. Shall we have some bacon too?"

Jasper rolled toward me, stretched his arms, and placed one over my body as he snuggled close to me. He lifted his head to see our son.

"Bacon sounds yummy to me." He kissed me on the cheek. "Good morning. I'll start the bacon and you mix up the pancakes and make the coffee. Deal?"

I sighed as I could not help but smile.

"Deal."

The children set the table and retrieved the orange juice from the refrigerator as Jasper and I prepared breakfast. I closed my eyes as the first bite of buttery pancake drenched with real maple syrup tantalized my taste buds.

"This is so good," Maysie said with her mouth full of pancake.

I nodded as I swallowed.

"I agree, but we don't talk with our mouth full of food. It's impolite."

I watched the children's faces as they enjoyed their breakfast, fully aware that someday they would become independent and no longer reside within our home. For today, I would enjoy and treasure this moment.

After washing the breakfast dishes, I upheld my promise by retrieving my journal, dating, and jotting down my latest vision. On a whim, I called my sister-in-law.

"Good morning."

"Hi. I had a vision of a baby boy who will be born during the winter."

"Interesting. You do have a gift for visions."

"Yes, are you expecting?"

"A baby?"

"Yes."

"If I am, it's news to me."

The vision haunted my mind over the next few months. I was certain my sister-in-law would be expecting her second child soon.

***

My brother, his wife, and son entered our house dressed in their red, white, and blue for attending our town's annual Fourth of July parade. I could no longer contain my suspicion as I glanced at her stomach before speaking.

"Ok, I had a dream a few months ago about a baby sleeping in a crib and I can't get it out of my mind. There was a giant hand that lifted the baby out of the crib. It was wearing a dark blue velvet sleeper, as dark as the night sky, and it was decorated with snowflakes. I assume a baby boy will be born during the winter months." I looked from my brother to his wife as they looked at each other and remained speechless.

She smiled at him nodding her approval. He looked at me and grinned.

"We are expecting a baby in February. We weren't going to tell anyone yet because she is only eight weeks along."

"I knew it! That's wonderful news." I hugged them both.

My brother looked at me narrowing his eyes.

"So, another boy, huh?"

"Assuming the dark blue sleeper indicates the gender, I guess we will see if your 'little bairn' is a boy when you have the ultrasound done, or aren't you going to find out until he is born?"

"We haven't discussed that yet, but I assume we will want to know the gender so we can prepare for 'his' arrival."

"You will want to know what?" Jasper entered the room with the children scooting past him to greet their cousin.

"We were just talking about finding out the gender of our baby when we have the ultrasound done. We are due in February." My brother announced.

"You're expecting. Congrats."

"Da, it's time to go." Maysie tugged on Jasper's shorts eager to be on our way. The children were loaded into wagons and we walked into town to set out our chairs and eat breakfast at the community center before watching the parade.

* * *

In February, my brother's family increased by one as they welcomed their baby boy. Like most families, we gathered to celebrate the occasion with heartfelt congratulations, gifts, and food, always food. Grandma insisted on having a photo session with countless pictures taken with all four of her great-grandchildren. The children did a good job of sitting still, but toward the end, the baby cried, and the others became restless.

Our family dinners have become a little chaotic with eight of us in attendance. Occasionally Grandma attends too, but I think the noise of the little ones is sometimes too much for her to handle. I often sit at the kitchen table and laugh at the children's antics and am thankful we are together, happy, and healthy. I often wonder if Dad is watching over us, guiding us through life. As forewarned by Mom, I do not find feathers anymore.

*　*　*

We gathered at my brother's house in celebration of his oldest son's fourth birthday. Everyone was in attendance, including Grandma and my sister-in-law's parents.

My brother carried his youngest from the kitchen into the living room. He set the one-and-a-half-year-old on my lap.

"Can you watch this mischievous little guy for a few minutes. He keeps trying to stick his fingers in the birthday cake."

"Sure." I tried to entertain him by playing pattycake, but the game did not hold his interest. He slithered like a snake from my lap and ran away.

"Get back here." I stood to chase after him as he hid around the side of the couch. I waited and watched him peek around the corner. He giggled as he played peek-a-boo with me.

"I see you." I teased as I took a step toward him.

His eyes became large and a smile grew on his face. He scrunched his shoulders upward toward his head and raised his hand wiggling his fingers at me.

"Bye-bye." He ran into the hallway expecting me to chase him.

UNTIL WE MEET AGAIN

I froze in place as an eerie feeling passed through my body from head to toe. A memory perhaps, of a person, that I loved dearly, whose similar wave was captured in many of the pictures in the photo albums I had at home and framed on my desk. I stared at my nephew's retreating little body as he ran away. *Mom?*

I hope you enjoyed reading

Until We Meet Again.

If so, your review on Amazon.com

would be greatly appreciated.

For further information about

Brenda Hasse Books,

please visit

www.BrendaHasseBooks.com.

www.ingramcontent.com/pod-product-compliance
Lightning Source LLC
Chambersburg PA
CBHW031107080526
44587CB00011B/871